Richard W. Hill

The BOSS

The BOSS

Published by
PYRAMID MEDIA GROUP
666 Fifth Avenue, Suite 230, New York, NY 10103, USA
Tel: +1212 713-5077 • Fax: +1212 315-1534
Europe
2 Route du Grand Lancy, Geneva , CH 1227, Switzerland
Tel: +4122 343-1111 • Fax: +4122 343-0220
Email: info@pyramid.ch
Web: www.PyramidMediaGroup.com & www.pyramid.ch

IBSN 0-944188-19-2

Printed in Switzerland

Contents

Richard W. Hill

The BOSS

Machiavelli on Managerial Leadership

PYRAMID MEDIA GROUP

New York • Geneva

Preface

For almost five centuries politicians and political scientists have studied a little book by a diplomat of the tiny republic of Florence (population about one-hundred thousand). Entitled *Il Principe* (roughly translated as *The Prince*), Niccolò Machiavelli's book tells how various bold leaders gained and held power in the city-states of Renaissance Italy. Thus its subject is political leadership. Its method is close observation of reality. Machiavelli's observations are illustrated and reinforced by historical examples. The hard-headed author rejects theories based on mere tradition or pure speculation.

First as a student, then later as a manager, I noticed that Machiavelli's observations about political leadership apply equally to other kinds of leadership, especially business leadership. That idea led me to apply key parts of *Il Principe* to business management. Machiavelli's observations fit the business world so neatly that I have entitled my adaptation *The Boss*. My arrangement of topics in *The Boss* follows fairly closely the order of chapters in the original book.

In each of my twenty-three chapters, I start with an adaptation of Machiavelli's observations on a vital topic or set of topics. Then I make comments and raise questions about the application of Machiavellian principles to modern business. My comments and questions are illustrated and reinforced by real-life cases, sprinkled with observations by current authorities on business leadership.

Postscript:
Machiavelli's Life and Times

attain and hold power, without regard to moral, ethical, or religious principles that might conflict with the attainment of power. Machiavelli observes that, at times, a ruler acting in the best interests of his state might need to violate commonly accepted canons of behavior for individuals.

In the same way, managers must at times act in ways that would not be condoned on the part of employees.

While Machiavelli's observations are based on a close observation of reality, he himself appears motivated by an idealistic view of the use of power: to improve the position of a state with respect to its competitors and potential enemies. Thus Machiavelli's writing can be considered optimistic, in contract to the bleak pessimism that characterizes an equally realistic work: George Orwell's *Nineteen Eighty-four*. Orwell describes the horror that ensues when rulers pursue power as an end in itself, rather than for the sake of a collective goal. "The Party seeks power entirely for its own sake," says O'Brien as he tortures Winston. "We are not interested in the good of others; we are interested solely in power. ... Power is not a means, it is an end. ... The object of persecution is persecution. The object of torture is torture. The object of power is power." Machiavelli would have been chilled by such a thought.

Indeed, Machiavelli observes that a successful leader must:
- possess expert knowledge in the area that is most important for the success of his or her organization;

The reader can see that my preface stresses *leadership* rather than *management*. I have chosen this emphasis to reflect the thrust of Machiavelli's book and to address what I believe to be the main failing of the large modern corporation. *The Boss* is not about managerial techniques such as centralization versus decentralization, delegation, or span of control but rather is about the qualities of leadership. An astute leader, as Machiavelli implies, can master managerial techniques, or hire and motivate needed experts, whereas even a brilliant manager (sometimes called a "technocrat") can fall short as a leader.

Today's competitive business environment puts as much pressure on would-be leaders as did the fiercely competitive political environment of Renaissance Italy. Only the scale has changed. Instead of facing a dozen or so rival city-states in Italy, modern business leaders confront hundreds of competitors around the world. Today's global economy includes eager competitors in the former socialist states and the emerging Third World, not to mention those in the Asian "Tigers" and the developed countries. All the players, moreover, have access to a bewildering array of technological advances, in production techniques, in quality control, in transportation, and in telecommunications. Machiavelli would undoubtedly have relished the challenge. Since we cannot sit down with him, we can learn from his most famous book.

Machiavelli's work is descriptive rather than normative. That is, he describes what must be done in practice in order to

- be skilled at knowing when and how to use this expert knowledge;
- have some luck.

While the role of luck is undeniable, its importance can be reduced by appropriate behavior, and Machiavelli discusses this point in depth.

Some years ago, a state legislature in the United States passed a law declaring that the ratio of the circumference of a circle to its diameter was 3.0 in that state, rather than 3.1416... as elsewhere. The purpose of the law was to facilitate life for the young students of geometry in the state. Needless to say, the law failed.

Just as the laws of nature cannot be ignored or repealed, so Machiavelli's maxims cannot be ignored or repealed, and successful managers follow them, consciously or unconsciously, willingly or unwillingly.

Success in a competitive environment cannot be achieved without behaving in a way that is adapted to the pressures of the environment: this is the essential message that Machiavelli bequeaths to us from the 15th and 16th centuries. As we read his maxims, we can see whether his observations are as illuminating to us in the business world as they have been to leaders of the political world since 1513.

Introduction: What Can We Learn From Machiavelli?

I.   The Nature of Machiavelli's Advice

Politicians and political scientists have studied the writing of Niccolò Machiavelli for almost five centuries. Indeed his short book *Il Principe*, written in 1513, is widely recognized as the first textbook on practical politics. *Il Principe* has been the subject of lively controversy from the first pirated handwritten copies to the printed editions in virtually every language. Machiavelli's book has been damned as immoral, cynical, pessimistic, and wicked, while being praised as realistic, scientific, unsentimental, and honest.

The title itself, *Il Principe*, arouses misunderstanding. The usual English translation, *The Prince*, suggests a hereditary ruler. But that is not Machiavelli's topic. His subject is the strong leader who maneuvered his way to the top of a city-state in Renaissance Italy: whether a soldier, a priest, a merchant, or an aristocrat. Although Machiavelli favored the republican form of government - provided the state has a virtuous citizenry - he accepted any form of government, including monarchy, if well led. While he preferred cultivated leaders - and recognized that hereditary leaders enjoyed the advantage of continuity - his emphasis was on strong leadership.

Il Principe is a textbook for those who aspire to positions of political leadership. It contains advice on all the major

challenges that a would-be leader can expect to encounter. Machiavelli's advice broke new ground-ground that is still being tilled. Instead of deducing rules of behavior from religious or philosophical assumptions about human nature, Machiavelli based his advice on close observation of leaders. His observations were made during fourteen years' service in the foreign office of the Republic of Florence, as diplomat abroad and civil servant at home. (How Machiavelli lost his post, and how that loss affected him, are described in Part II of this Introduction.) Since Machiavelli was a learned man, *Il Principe* uses many historical examples. These examples, however, are used to illustrate or reinforce the author's observations - not to establish assumptions. Thus Machiavelli's method departed from the classical and medieval deductive approach, and was in harmony with the inductive approach of the Renaissance - what we would call the case method in today's business schools.

In this sense, Machiavelli's method is scientific. Like a modern behavioral scientist, Machiavelli induced generalizations about human behavior from systematic observations. Of course he lacks some of the techniques of modern behavioral science, such as surveys and statistical analyses, and his work lacks the undergirding of modern psychological research. Nonetheless a remarkable number of Machiavelli's generalizations are supported by modern behavioral science.

Also like a modern behavioral scientist, Machiavelli avoids moral judgements in *Il Principe* (though not in his other books).

Here he tries to exclude moral and ethical considerations - what scientists call normative principles. Hence his focus is on achieving success as a leader, rather than on attaining moral excellence. (To be sure, Machiavelli cannot refrain from all moral judgements in *Il Principe*. In Chapter VIII, for example, he notes how "a man may get power" through "fearful cruelty and inhumanity" but not "glory" nor a place "among the really excellent men.") Another way to describe Il Principe is to mark its concern with the real world rather than an ideal one. It is Machiavelli's unflinching realism that offends many idealists. And it is his "scientific cynicism" that offends many moralists.

Two legitimate objections can be levelled against *Il Principe*. The first is Machiavelli's assumption that all human beings are naturally bad and motivated by unlimited selfishness. Such an assessment was impossible for Machiavelli to reach on the basis of his relatively limited observations or the accumulated knowledge of his time - and may indeed forever remain beyond the reach of science[1]. Thus Machiavelli's pessimistic premise of inherent human evil is as much a moral judgment as the optimistic premise of inherent human goodness.

---

[1] Thirty years ago, a team of psychologists made a detailed study of behaviors which they considered measures of ethical "soundness" among graduate students at the University of California. Their conclusion: "Our High Soundness subjects are beset, like all other persons, by fears, unrealizable desires, self-condemned hates, and tensions difficult to resolve. They are sound largely because they bear with their anxieties, hew to a stable course, and maintain some sense of the ultimate worthwhileness of their lives." Were these high achievers "good" or "bad"? See Creativity and Psychological Health by Frank Barron (Van Nostrand, 1963).

The second objection to *Il Principe* is that it does not envision a human order beyond that of the nation-state. In his concluding chapter, Machiavelli does foresee a unified Italy supplanting an assortment of city-states. Not surprisingly, however, he cannot foresee regional and global political and economic confederations like the European Union, the North American Free Trade Association, or the United Nations.

To some extent forecasts about the success of confederations in promoting human harmony depend on one's assumptions about human nature. People must at least be able, in the words of the US Constitution, "to form a more perfect union." Note, however, that the US Founding Fathers, like Machiavelli, accepted the Judeo-Christian belief in original sin. As Madison wrote in *The Federalist*: "If men were angels, no government would be necessary." Since they are not, he advised, "Ambition must be made to counteract ambitions."

Regardless of how much a manager's own world-view differs from Machiavelli's, he or she can learn much in *The Boss* about the qualities of strong, successful leadership.

II. The Source of Machiavelli's Advice

The air was still and humid, the heat was stifling in Rome on August 18, 1503. Pope Alexander VI, of the Borgia family, lay gravely ill. Those who could do so had moved to the cool green hills outside the city, to escape the furnace-like heat reflected off the ancient Roman monuments. But the rulers of Rome had not been able to leave, because foreign armies were marching nearby and the political situation was critical.

The sultry heat took its toll of those left in the city. For six days Pope Alexander had been fighting against a sudden fever, but, at the age of seventy-two, he was too old to win. He would die that night. His son, Cesare Borgia, *il Valentino*, formerly Archbishop and Cardinal of Valencia, now Duke of Valence, Captain General of the papal troops and Duke of Romagna, had fallen ill at the same time as Alexander, but had recovered just as the Pope died.

Enemies of the Borgias circulated the false rumor that Cesare had, by mistake, poisoned himself and his father while attempting to poison an unfriendly Cardinal. Many powerful politicians were pleased to believe the rumor. With the death of the Pope, Cesare's power base was eroded, and his brilliant and rapid climb to power was menaced.

For years, Niccolò Machiavelli, envoy of Florence, had observed Cesare, as he cunningly and skillfully used his and the Pope's resources to build a strong state in central Italy. Machiavelli had hoped and dreamed that Cesare would continue to gain power, and would become the ruler, *il principe*, who could unite Italy, and expel the foreign invaders. But fortune intervened, by causing Cesare to fall ill at the same time as his father, so that for six critical days no Borgia leaders were able to manage Roman affairs. And thus Machiavelli's dream faded, for he was too much of a realist to believe that Cesare could overcome this crisis.

Later, in October, Machiavelli was in Rome, to observe Cesare's struggle to maintain power. He reported to Florence that Cesare's position was weak, and that Florence should not support him. By this time Cesare's political situation was so hopeless that he was obliged to trust the promises of Giuliano della Rovere, soon to be Pope Julius II, a man whom he and Alexander had severely offended, a man who had every reason to be his mortal enemy.

The outcome was not surprising: in spite of his enemies' promises, Cesare wound up in prison, was forced to give up control of his troops and fortresses in Romagna, and was exiled to Spain. He was never again a factor in European politics. Pope Julius would go on to play a major role in the politics of the time, but he is best remembered as the sponsor of Michelangelo, who decorated the ceiling of Sixtine Chapel for him.

Chapter VII of *Il Principe* is devoted to Cesare's rise and fall, and to the lessons to be learned from it. They are summarized in sections 12 and 13 of the chapter:

> *There was in the Duke so much fierce valor and virtue, and he knew so well how men should be*

won or abandoned, ... that, if foreign armies had not been menacing him closely, or if he had been healthy, he won have sustained all difficulties. He told me himself, on the day that Julius II was elected, that he had thought of everything that could happen when his father died, and had found a solution to all problems, except that he had never thought that he himself could be gravely ill when his father died.

So I, having observed all the actions of the Duke, would not reproach him; rather I would propose him as an example to follow for all those who have climbed to power using fortune and the strength of others. ... The only opposition to his plans was the short length of Alexander's reign, and his own illness.

Therefore whoever believes it necessary, when coming into new power, to insure against enemies; to gain friends; to win by force or by fraud; to make oneself loved and feared by the people, obeyed and respected by the soldiers; to eliminate those that can and must harm you; to innovate old ways of doing things by introducing new ways; to be strict and fair, magnanimous and generous; to eliminate unfaithful troops; to raise new troops; to keep the friendship of Kings and Princes, so that they will either courteously help you or be cautious

> when offending you; whoever believes this, I
> say, cannot find better examples than the
> actions of Cesare Borgia.
>
> We can only reproach him regarding the
> election of Julius II ... because he should never
> have consented in the election of a man whom
> he had offended, and who feared him. ... For
> whoever believes that amongst powerful people
> new favours will lead to forgetting old insults is
> deluding himself. Thus in this election the Duke
> make a mistake, and it was the cause of his
> ultimate ruin[2].

Ten years after the dramatic events in Rome, in 1513, Machiavelli finished writing up the observations he had made as a diplomat, and presented the finished work to the man who had gained absolute power in Florence, Lorenzo dei Medici, a descendant of that Lorenzo justly known as Il Magnifico. Although Renaissance Florence was theoretically a republic, actual power shifted between the signoria and the Medici family. The signoria were chiefly businessmen who had anointed themselves as aristocrats. Since Machiavelli had been a civil servant under the signoria, he was suspect to the Medici. he hoped that his treatise, Il Principe, would gain him the favour of Lorenzo. Here are the words that he used to present his work to the new ruler:

---

[2] A very readable and accurate account of the rise and fall of the Borgias (including the life of Cesare's sister, the unjustly maligned Lucrezia Borgia) is given by Michael Mallet in The Borgias (Granada, 1981).

Those who wish to acquire the favour of a prince very often present to him those things which they hold dearest, or those things of which they see the prince to be fond; hence one often sees presents of horses, arms, cloth of gold, jewels and other ornaments worthy of the ruler's greatness.

Since I wish to offer myself to Your Magnificence with some proof of my fealty to you, I have not found amongst my possessions anything else that I hold dearer or more valuable than my knowledge of the actions of great men. This knowledge I have acquired through long experience of modern events and continuous study of ancient history. Having with great diligence, and at length, thought about and examined these facts, I have now reduced them into a small volume, which I offer to Your Magnificence.

And I hope that there can be no greater gift, than to give you the ability to learn in a very short time everything that I have seen and understood, during so many years, through so many uncomfortable and dangerous experiences.

The treatise did not restore Machiavelli to Florentine civil service, but it did bring him everlasting fame.

The modern business manager should benefit from his wisdom, which was indeed based on vast experience, acquired during the many years when he was Florence's ambassador (or more precisely observer, a non-speaking member of the embassy, a spy we might say today), visiting the courts of Italy and of Europe, including those of King Louis XII of France and of the Holy Roman Emperor Maximilian.

The extreme cynicism of *Il Principe*, especially the conviction that people are fundamentally selfish, should be understood as a consequence of the objective scientific spirit with which Machiavelli approaches his topic. This cold, impartial, almost inhuman objectivity, which considers events on their own merits, independently of most moral, ethical or religious conventions, divorced from wishes for the way things should be, rather than they way they are, was revolutionary for the time, and has been often misunderstood through the ages.

Machiavelli never said that *the end justifies* the means, or anything similar; that was a misinterpretation by English critics of the Victorian period. *The end justifies the means* is a moral judgement, and Machiavelli does not make moral judgements in *Il Principe*. Here Machiavelli is an observer of reality, who reports on what he sees, like a modern scientist. If we have to reduce Machiavelli's observations to one sentence, then we might say that he saw that *the end requires the means.*

Machiavelli cannot be accused of being unethical or immoral. He observed the behavior of those who gain and hold power, and reported on it. His conclusion, based on observation, is that successful rulers acting in the best interests of their states might need to violate commonly accepted canons of behavior for individuals. He would certainly extend that conclusion from leaders of states to leaders (as opposed to mere administrators) of all large organizations.

Machiavelli would certainly not have condoned the reckless behavior of those businessman who believe that they are above the law. Such behavior can only lead to ruin, for it is nothing less than offending someone (society as a whole) whose vengeance you have every reason to fear. And, as Machiavelli wrote in *Il Principe*: *"If you offend someone, do it in such a way that you need not fear his revenge"*. In another book, he gave a more direct warning: *"Both people and princes err when they are not controlled by laws."*[3]

Proper understanding and application of Machiavelli's maxims in the business world would result in less illegal and socially destructive behavior, and would have helped the arbitrage and junk-bond kings of Wall Street to avoid over-reaching themselves, and plunging to ruin.

III. Machiavelli's Advice as Presented in This Book

In order to facilitate the application of Machiavelli's observations to today's business world, I have freely substituted

---

[3] From Discourses on *Titus Livius*, Book I, Chapter 38. In Book III, Chapter 5, he wrote: "[Princes] begin to lose their states at that hour when they begin to break the laws and those customs and usages... under which men have lived for a long time."

business-related words for words related to the politics of Renaissance states. Thus I have chosen the colloquial term boss to express what Machiavelli expressed as *principe*. Even in terms of the politics of states, Machiavelli's term expresses a somewhat different concept than the English *prince*. As explained above, Machiavelli's term can apply to a strong leader who is not a prince in the aristocratic sense. It can apply to a weak leader who inherits power as well as to a person who attains power thanks to some fortuitous circumstances.

The terms *manager* or *leader* could convey the same meaning as *principe*. I prefer *boss* because, as noted before, my emphasis is on those managers who are also leaders. Some other consistent substitutions of terms are *organization* for *state*, *employees* for the *citizenry* of a state, and so forth.

With few exceptions, I have avoided consistent use of *"his or her"* and *"he or she"* in place of *his* or *he*, in order to avoid lengthening the text. The reader is encouraged to keep in mind that *his* and *he* apply equally to managers who are female.

In Machiavelli's text, each enunciation of a maxim is followed by one or more historical examples. Since these examples are not directly related to modern business, I have replaced them. The replacement consists of examples drawn from my experience of modern business, of case reports from various sources, and of observations and questions intended to encourage the reader to supply examples based on his or her personal experience. I hope that thinking of examples will help you to apply Machiavelli's wisdom to your experience.

Each of the following chapters contains a loose translation of Machiavelli's text, indented and set in italic type. The excerpt is ended by a parenthesized reference to the original chapter and section in *Il Principe*. My comments and questions are in regular type. Examples, including case reports, are indented and set in helvetic type.

I hope you will have as much fun pondering what follows as I have had in putting it together.

The Boss

Machiavelli on Managerial Leadership

1. Seeking and Holding Power

People change boss willingly, in the belief that the new one will be better. But in this they deceive themselves, because later with experience they see that they are worse off.

(III-1)

If you are still on the way up, how often have you wished that top management would replace "the incompetent" who is your boss? (In a recent survey of middle managers, a business magazine found that only 38% were favorable toward the ability of top management.[3]) But how often is your new boss worse than the old one?

In a sales organization where I once worked, the sales manager - I'll call him "Hale" - was easygoing and undisciplined. Morale was lukewarm, and everyone believed that mediocre sales resulted from Hale's loose control. Higher management shared our view and replaced Hale with "Queeg," a high-flyer with an accounting background and a reputation for running a tight ship.

After the honeymoon, morale plummeted below its previous low point, and sales did not improve. Everyone realized that Hale's style had not been the problem and that a change to Queeg's style was not the solution. The problem turned out to be that the target market demanded products and services which could not be easily provided by our sales organization, because of the overall structure and objectives of the corporation to which we belonged. Fortunately top management began to make the necessary changes before our organization went under. There upon we all resolved to quit making a scapegoat of our boss. Instead, we adapted our behavior to Queeg's style so that he relaxed and behaved more like Hale.

As Machiavelli says:

When you acquire authority over a department whose functions, culture, or organization are dissimilar from those of the departments you already manage, you will need great luck and hard work in order to assert your authority. One of the best techniques is for you to involve yourself personally in managing the new department.

Because, if you manage personally, you will see problems as they arise, and can correct them at once; if you are not personally involved, you will learn of problems only when they are

---

[4] Fortune, 18 November 1991, survey of 750'000 middle managers by Hay Research for Management. The percentage approving their superiors' ability had declined from 54% in 1985-1987.

> serious, and can no longer be corrected. In
> addition, if you manage personally, the new
> department will not be neglected or raided by
> your subordinates. (III-4)

Have you noticed how often a trusted employee of "Company A" has the good luck to become "acting" manager when his or her firm takes over "Company B"? Luck may give you the opportunity to expand your power, but only personal involvement will hold your new domain.

> I have experienced several mergers and
> acquisitions. In every case, trusted employees
> of the acquiring company were given authority
> over key functions of the acquired company.
> But I know of a case in book publishing where a
> new acting manager failed to consolidate his
> position. Prosperous Company A took over poor
> but clever Company B. A junior executive of
> Company A was made acting manager of
> Company B's innovative textbook division.
> Instead of becoming personally involved, the
> Company A man spent a month visiting
> glamorous yet unimportant overseas markets,
> leaving the old Company B manager in charge.
> When the globe-trotter returned, he found that
> top management had given his position to the
> former subordinate from the downtrodden
> Company B.

> *Another good solution is to colonize the new organization. (III-5)*

Did you ever notice how often new managers replace old department heads with new department heads that have previously worked with them? These bosses are "colonizing" their new organizations. A new boss doesn't necessarily choose his top subordinates from his old shop. He chooses "up-and-coming" types who share his latest thinking about their kind of enterprise.

> *A spectacular example occurred in one organization that I once worked for. A newly appointed top manager immediately replaced all five department heads reporting to him. His five appointees came from throughout the industry and had shown their harmony with his thinking, expressed in articles and professional meetings. The new managerial team "colonized" the organization, planting and cultivating the boss's ideas.*

Machiavelli again:

> *Here we must notice that people must be either indulged or eliminated, because they will take revenge for small offenses, but cannot for serious ones. So if you offend someone, do it in such a way that you do not fear his revenge. (III-5)*

Undoubtedly, you have seen a new manager accept objectionable behavior from an "inherited" subordinate. Why

27

does a boss do so? Very likely the boss is indulging a crusty old veteran because replacement would be inconvenient while antagonism would be costly.

> *I saw a newly appointed first-line supervisor put up with extremely hostile behavior from the long-term department secretary, because he needed to rely on her inside information until he became familiar with his new domain.*

Did you ever see a boss's projects being sabotaged by someone that he or she has offended, perhaps unknowingly, in the dim past? If you are a new boss and feel sure that one of your subordinates holds a grudge against you, then firing that subordinate is your best option. If that is not feasible, you should try to arrange a "lateral promotion" so that the subordinate can no longer take revenge by obstructing your projects.

> *In one case that I observed, "Heep" accepted his new boss, "Copperfield," as better qualified to be department manager, but could not forgive him for a defeat in tennis eleven years before. For reasons of corporate politics, Copperfield could not fire Heep. But suddenly another department had an urgent need for a "Special Projects Manager"; top management spotted Heep as the obvious candidate for this job. A company wag said that he saw Copperfield's "fine Italian hand" (Machiavellian?) in the convenient "lateral promotion."*

Machiavelli again:

He who has authority over a non-homogeneous organization must become leader and protector of the less powerful neighbors, and find ways to weaken the powerful leaders of the organization, and watch out that no outsider as powerful as himself acquires authority in the organization by some chance event.

Because it happens that, as soon as a powerful outsider acquires authority, all the less powerful members of the organization join the outsider, pushed by the jealousy that they have against whoever had power over them. (III-6)

Did you ever observe a department paralyzed when the weaker employees back a newly arrived manager from outside, venting their envy of a tried-and-true leader?

In one high-technology company, I saw the drudges welcome the hotshot from outside - I'll call him "Flashman" - out of jealousy toward tried-and-true "Rockford." The two were assistant chief engineers, with equally important responsibilities. Work was severely hindered by the drudges' favoritism toward Flashman. The chief engineer could not stop the spitefulness, so Rockford quit, depriving the company of a potential top manager. Flashman also quit later on. Like many competent middle

> *managers, Rockford was unskilled in organizational politics and was thus vulnerable to the threat from Flashman's magnetism. Companies would benefit by teaching their "Rockfords" how to protect themselves from their "Flashmans."*

This behavior can be particularly insidious for certain types of "matrix-management" organizations. In my experience, matrix-management works well when the lines of authority are clearly separate and synergy is created. For example, a project to develop a high-technology product, in which the project manager exercises overall control, while specialist department heads (aerodynamics, materials, fabrication, etc.) supervise only for their specialty the engineers assigned to the project. The project benefits from the combined wisdom of all concerned managers. Matrix management works poorly when lines of authority overlap and appear to be politically motivated, for example dual reporting to regional and headquarters managers who have the same functional specialization and work hard to impose their views only so that they can assert their own personal power.

> *We can say of managing a difficult situation what physicians say of disease: in the early stages it is easy to cure and hard to recognize, while, with time, if it hasn't been found and treated, it becomes easy to recognize and hard to cure. (III-8)*

How many times have you seen a situation degenerate until top management finally became aware of the problem and was forced to take drastic action? How often could the problem have been fixed more easily if action had been taken sooner?

> *In another high-tech company's research department that I observed, the problem was not the quality of the work but simply the department's inability to generate timely reports. The situation degenerated until top management found the reporting delays unacceptable. At that point, drastic action was taken: writers and supervisors were hired; information processing equipment was doubled. In retrospect, it can be seen that a minor investment in training and equipment - made a few years earlier - would have avoided the problem.*

As Machiavelli puts it:

> *The following general rule is never or rarely wrong: whoever is the reason for someone else attaining power will come to ruin; because that power was given either through cleverness or through brute force, and both of these are suspect to whoever has become powerful.*
> *(III-14).*

Did you ever see a newly promoted manager proceed to put aside precisely those people who helped him to achieve the new rank?

In a corporate reorganization that I observed, a matrix-managed structure was realigned so that central control was stronger. The new top manager who emerged was the magisterial "Lyon," although the change had been engineered by the wily "Fox" in collaboration with the forceful "Baer." One of Lyon's first moves was to force Fox and Baer to leave. (In a study of a technology-based manufacturing firm, a Harvard Business School team found that the power gained by someone promoting change "stems in large measure from the multiple sources of authority attached to his position in the structure."[5]) Neither cleverness nor forcefulness alone is enough.

---

[5] Gene W. Dalton, Louis B. Barnes, and Abraham Zaleznik, The Distribution of Power in Formal Organization (Division of Research, Harvard Business School, 1968).

2. Taking Charge of Centralized and Decentralized Organizations: A Study in Contrasts

> *If you think about centralized and decentralized organizations, you will find that centralized organizations are difficult to take over, but, once taken over, easy to manage. On the contrary, decentralized organizations are in some ways easier to take over, but more difficult to manage after they are taken over. (IV-2)*

Did you ever try to assert authority over a highly centralized department? Did your formal grant of authority by top management put you in control? Or did you need to overcome resistance?

> *In my own career as a manager, I once took charge of a highly centralized department. The departing department head (nicknamed "Mr. Efficiency") ran a tight ship, with no errors in operations and with a loyal crew. I saw that his weakness was in navigation: in the direction he was leading the department. Mr. Efficiency emphasized speed and cost-reduction while overlooking customer-satisfaction. My task was to convince department members of Mr. Efficiency's shortcomings. Doing so took all my*

skill at persuasion. Once I had done so, however, my new subordinates accepted my leadership unquestioningly (and Mr. Efficiency's early retirement helped). An innovative manager gains support "in proportion to his power and the relevance of his power to the objectives of the organization"[6]).

Compare my experience with your own. Did you ever take over a highly centralized department? Does Machiavelli describe the process accurately? Now consider the reverse situation: a highly decentralized department.

In a contrasting case that I observed, a new manager took over a department that was highly decentralized geographically, with a strong matrix management organization in local branches. The new manager ("Steerforth") wanted to impose more centralized functional control and more uniformity in procedures. Although Steerforth at first had no trouble in asserting his authority, he needed more than five years to put his reorganization into effect. He had to convince the geographically dispersed department members that his reorganization was relevant to the corporation's goals.

6 Gene W. Dalton, Louis B. Barnes, and Abraham Zaleznik, The Distribution of Power in Formal Organization (Division of Research, Harvard Business School, 1968).

Observing a similar case, Dalton et al. quote Michael Crozier: "Resistance to changes occurs when the effect of change is to alter the balance of power within the organization without offsetting compensations." As a promoter of change, Steerforth had to sell his subordinates on the payoffs from his reorganization. Doing so took time and effort.

3. How to Take Charge of Departments Accustomed to Being Run in Their Own Particular Ways

Should you acquire authority over departments that have been used to their own rules and independence, you have three ways to manage them: 1) destroy them; 2) manage them personally; 3) let them continue to operate under their own rules, establishing inside the department a few people who will keep it friendly to you. Because these few people will have been promoted by you, the boss, they will know that they will not survive without your protection, and they will do everything to keep it. (V-1)

Did you ever watch other managers fail miserably when they tried to impose new operating rules on a department that had been independent for a long time? Did they take one of the above three approaches?

In one case that I observed in the recorded music business, a marketing manager, "Wiseman," was given authority over the customer service department. Formerly this department had, quite irrationally, reported in a loose way to the controller. The department was headed by "Spalding," a favorite golf partner of the Chief Executive Officer - and also of the largest customers. Spalding's department was cost-efficient and smoothly run. Unfortunately, however, customer service sometimes failed to digest and transmit accurate marketing information about record content or playing schedules.

Wiseman wisely rejected the option of "destroying" customer service (Machiavelli's technique number 1) by merging it with marketing, since he wanted to avoid unnecessarily offending important customers and the Chief Executive Officer. Instead, his solution was to give Spalding two new assistants: "Copland," a near-genius with music, and "Ricky," a fanatic on schedules - this is Machiavelli's technique number 3.

Why, the reader may ask, did not Wiseman confront Spalding about correcting his department's deficiency (Machiavelli's technique number 2)? Obviously he sensed that Spalding's ambition was not strong enough to motivate change in his ways. Human ambition (or motivation to achieve) varies considerably, as experimental psychologists have shown.[7]

As Machiavelli says:

> *But, in truth, there is no sure way to manage a previously independent department except to destroy it. And if you become the boss of a department used to its independence, and you do not thoroughly reorganize it, you can expect to fail to assert your authority.*
>
> *Because anyone who does not wish to obey orders will always invoke independence and the old ways of doing things, which are never forgotten. And no matter what you do, if you do not reorganize or replace the employees, they will never forget the old ways of doing things, and will always invoke them whenever there are problems. (V-3)*

How often do marketplace changes induced by technological process force significant internal change? The latest buzzword for these phenomena appears to be "corporate re-engineering": the concept of redefining internal operating procedures in order to better meet customer requirements through the application of new technologies.

How often has it been necessary to completely reorganize a previously independent department in order to assure that it complies with some new organization or some new operating rules? Have you seen such cases?

---

[7] See for example Achievement Motivation in Perspective (Academic Press, 1985) by Heinz Heckhausen of Germany's Max Planck Institute.

In the previous example, Wiseman succeeded in exerting managerial control over a formerly quasi-independent department because Spalding's ambition was limited. Hence Wiseman was able to "colonize" the customer service department with his people (Copland and Ricky). The situation would have been very different if Spalding had retired and been replaced by a highly-ambitious Ricky, supported by Copland.

Such a situation occurred in my experience. In that case, a changing business environment forced the company to reorganize to become "leaner and meaner," despite the ambitions of department heads. The Chief Executive Officer was forced to be tough. Subordinate department managers were continually obstructing the new approach, which involved more central control. They claimed that only the old approach was valid, and that anyway they only worked well when they were independent, and not subject to central control.

Eventually, top management prevailed, but only after several years of bitter corporate in-fighting, which resulted in the more-or-less forced departure of several old-time middle managers.

4. On Acquiring New Authority Through One's Own Skill - Plus Luck

If we look at the lives and actions of great leaders, we see that they had nothing more from fortune than a chance to assert their leadership; ... without luck their skills would have been wasted, and without their skills the chance would have been wasted. (VI-3)

Did you ever notice how neither luck nor ability alone is enough for success? How many managers can you think of who know how to use their skills to turn a bit of luck into a major success?

Most of my own business acquaintances will freely tell you about the lucky set of circumstances that got them started on their successful careers. And I know a couple of failures who had a break but not the skill to exploit it.

Cases abound of entrepreneurs who had the good luck to encounter timely inventions or marketing techniques, on which they built industrial enterprises such as General Electric, RCA, or McDonald's. But cases also abound of failures like those of Studebaker Automobiles or Eastern Airlines. Shakespeare expressed Machiavelli's observation in poetic terms:

"... Best are those

Whose blood and judgement are so well commingled

That they are not a pipe for fortune's finger

To sound what stop she pleases

> *Those who have become bosses through their own skill, acquiring authority with difficulty, retain authority easily: indeed, the difficulties that they have to acquire authority come in part from new ideas and methods that they are obliged to introduce in order to attain authority.*
>
> *One must consider that there is nothing more difficult to manage, nor more uncertain of success, nor more dangerous to handle, than to become a leader and to introduce a new way of doing things.*
>
> *Because the innovator has as enemies all those who benefit from the old ways, and is only weakly supported by those who would gain from the new ways.*
>
> *This weakness comes in part from fear of the enemies, who have the old their side, in part from the incredulity of people, who do not really believe in new things, unless they are the fruit of a real experience. (VI-5)*
>
> *But to discuss this subject in depth, it is necessary to see if the innovators are independent, or if they depend on others; that*

is, if in order to accomplish their work they need to ask, or if they can assert authority.

If they need to ask, they will always come to no good, and never accomplish anything; but when they are independent and can assert authority, then it is rare that they will fail.

Because people are inconsistent, and it is easy to convince them of something, but difficult to hold them to that conviction. Hence it is best to be organized so that when they no longer believe, they can be forced to believe. (VI-6)

How many innovations have had to be pushed through, in the end, by brute force, in spite of extensive persuasion beforehand?

Note that Machiavelli does not state that asserting authority is enough. Innovation will also fail if it is imposed from above without first building a consensus. What Machiavelli says is that both consensus-building and assertion of authority are necessary in most cases.

Personally, I have never seen any significant change happen without both extensive consensus-building and assertion of authority. The consensus-building prepares people to accept the imposition of authority. But they won't change the way they work unless they are forced to. A recent study of chief executives indicates that the overwhelming majority favor participative management, an essential condition for consensus-building.[8] But it also shows that CEOs are people of strong convictions. Above all, top management's authority depends on a record of success. In the words of Abraham Zaleznik, a psychologist at the Harvard Business School: "... hierarchical authority must prove its effectiveness of it to retain itself."[9]

---

[8] See David L. Kutz et al., CEO: Who Gets to the Top in America (Michigan State University, 1989).

[9] In Gene W. Dalton, Louis B. Barnes, and Abraham Zaleznik, The Distribution of Power in Formal Organization (Division of Research, Harvard

5. On Acquiring New Authority Through the Skills of Others - Plus Luck

Those who solely by fortune become bosses, become so with little effort, but remain so with considerable effort. They have no difficulty along the way, because they fly along it: but all the difficulties start once they arrive. (VII-1)

Did you ever observe someone grimly hanging on to a job at all costs, because he or she was incapable of getting any other job at the same level?

Over the years, I have seen three or four cases like that. Mediocrities became middle managers because of family or old-school ties to the big boss. But the wheel of fortune kept turning, bringing difficult challenges. The unfortunate individuals in those positions wound up spending all their time and energy on preserving their job security, and no time on actually getting the job done. In the end, every one was fired, or moved to a "Special Projects Manager" position.

As Machiavelli put it:

Such people depend on the goodwill and fate of whoever promoted them, and these are two very volatile and unstable things. They do not know how to be and cannot remain bosses. They don't

> *know because, unless they are individuals of great intelligence and skill, it is not reasonable that, never having exercised power, they should know how to lead. They cannot remain bosses because they have no friends and allies in the organization. ... Thus the first adversity destroys them. (VII-2)*

Can the reader recall some brilliant star (perhaps an MBA from a "prestige" school) propelled into a top spot, with disappointing results?

> *I know several such cases. In one instance, a systems analyst with no previous supervisory experience was placed in a high-level management job (managing managers). After much personal frustration, the individual asked for, and obtained, a lower-level job (supervising clerical workers). He was lucky, because his sponsor was still in power. Otherwise, he might have been treated less well.*
>
> As Machiavelli says:
>
> *Whoever thinks that recent favours will make powerful people forget old insults is fooling himself. (VII-14)*

Did you ever wonder why somebody was put aside in spite of good recent results?

In one case that I know of, an individual had very successfully completed a difficult assignment, turning an operation around completely from failure to success. He was the obvious candidate for a higher-level job that had just become available. He was refused the promotion because, years earlier, he had offended a very senior manager: at a staff meeting, he had expressed doubt about the technical know-how of this influential manager.

6. On Those Who Become Bosses Through Evil Actions - Compared with NecessaryToughness

But, because one can become a boss also through evil ways, two examples will be shown, without discussing the merits of this approach. (VIII-1)

Machiavelli gives two case histories. In one instance, a Renaissance princeling gained control of a city-state by trickery and cruelty. But he was in turn tricked and killed by citizens who considered his cruelty excessive. In the other case, in ancient times, a prince gained and held power through cruelty. Although Machiavelli considers the second ruler's cruelty excessive (not deserving "glory"), he is forced to conclude that this prince used his cruelty effectively. Thus, as the present book's introduction makes clear, Machiavelli is by no means a cynic who condones evil. Rather, he is a realist who recognizes that some cruelty - we moderns would say "toughness" - may be necessary behavior for bosses. Can you think of anyone who has moved up in the world through trickery or excessive toughness?

Daily news reports are filled with cases of individuals who have built successful careers on trickery and excessive toughness. Innocent people are constantly tricked out of their creations (inventions and ideas) and their possessions (ranging from small nesteggs to everything they own). And people are constantly subjected to unnecessary toughness: unwarranted foreclosures, called loans, layoffs, plant-closings, and so forth. Perpetrators of trickery and excessive toughness may or may not prosper - may end up on Park Avenue or in the penitentiary (or both successively) - though none would deserve glory in Machiavaelli's book. On the other hand, necessary toughness is another matter.

Here is what Machiavelli says:

When a boss takes over an organization, he should calculate what injuries he must do. Then injuries must be administered all at once, so that, being less visible, they will offend less. And favours must be done little by little, so that they will be more visible.

And, above all, the boss must not be forced to act by any favorable or unfavorable accident: because, if unfavorable circumstances force an action, you will be too late; and any good that you do will not help you, because it will be held to be forced on you, and your efforts will not be appreciated. (VIII-8)

Here are some questions to ponder. When companies are obliged to lay people off, is it better to lay off many people all at once, or a few at a time? Is reacting to emergencies an effective form of management? Do employees appreciate actions, favorable or unfavorable, taken by management as reactions to emergencies?

Many years ago, an organization that I worked for acquired another company. At first management over-optimistically thought that all employees could be absorbed. Then circumstances forced some to be laid off. Then some more had to be let go. At the end, the few who were left - the hard-core of talent from the acquired firm - were totally fed up with the acquiring company and found jobs elsewhere. They would have stayed if the acquiring management had taken consistent tough action from the beginning, rather than being forced to react to circumstances.

7. On Being a Boss in Oligarchic or Democratic Organizations

> *To become boss thanks to the favour of one's colleagues one needs either the favour of all the people or the favour of the leaders (and to succeed it is not necessary to have either great skills or great luck, but rather astuteness aided by luck). (IX-1)*

Machiavelli has a bias towards democracy, as noted in the Introduction, but is not sentimental about it. He recognizes two obstacles to democracy. For one thing, democracy requires informed voters, who are not always present. For another thing, historical circumstances often put democracy beyond human imagination. When democracy is not possible, people must make the best of oligarchy. Most modern business organizations are oligarchies because they cannot overcome the two obstacles to democracy cited by Machiavelli - in the opinion of their boards of directors.

Can the reader think of exceptions - or of prospects for change? Machiavelli here, as in Chapters 1, 4, and 5, shows his political realism. His formula for political success is luck plus astuteness. The successful boss doesn't necessarily have the greatest know-how or the greatest luck, but rather the right mix. Can the reader this of examples?

> *The authority of a boss stems either from the power of all employees or from that of the*

> *managers. ... Leaders appoint one of themselves*
> *boss, so that they can satisfy their appetites*
> *under his shadow. He who becomes boss with*
> *the help of other managers has greater difficulty*
> *in managing than he who becomes boss with*
> *the help of all employees; because he is a boss*
> *surrounded by many who seem to be his equals,*
> *and because of this he cannot command them*
> *and manage them in his own way. (IX-2)*

Does the reader believe there is a great deal of deference among the top managers and within the board of directors or do the top brass act as though they are all equals?

> *In my experience, top management is a club.*
> *You enter the club because of your personality,*
> *not your performance. As Roger Ailes, media*
> *consultant to Ronald Reagan and others, points*
> *out, top management promotes people it likes.[10]*
> *So top managers make sure they act in such a*
> *way that they continue to be liked.*

Good results are normally necessary for an employee to be promoted. Above a certain level they are usually not sufficient. Consequently, "clubmanship" takes over, because, above a

---

[10] Roger Ailes, You are the Message: Getting What You Want by Being Who You Are (Doubleday, 1988).

[11] See Abraham Zaleznik, The Managerial Mystique: Restoring Leadership in Business (Harper and Row, 1989) and W. Edwards Deming, Out of the Crisis (MIT, 1986). Deming holds that two-way communication between management and workers is essential to both quality and quantity of output.

certain level, the behavior and results expected of a manager are too complex to be easily measured. (But, according to Harvard's Zaleznik, leadership behavior can be measured, and so can managerial results, according to quality-guru Deming, the American who advised Japanese industry during its post-war recovery and now advises many US companies that "Quality is Job Number One."[11])

Since top-level managers cannot readily evaluate the results of their immediate subordinates, they tend to evaluate them on their personality and on behavior not directly related to results. As a consequence, large organizations tend to evolve management structures in which all managers think and behave in similar ways; non-conformist thoughts or behavior are discouraged.

Perhaps this is a major reason for the decline of productivity and competitiveness in the most developed countries, where large organizations control the majority of the production resources. Large organizations dominated by managers who all think alike tend to have difficulty adapting to changes in the external world: that is, they tend to adapt to market conditions more slowly than smaller companies, where the management structure is dynamic and subject to change.

A case in point is the US steel industry. The mammoth corporations, whose executives were comfortably accustomed to their smokestack technology, have had trouble competing in world markets. Not so for many small companies whose bosses immediately embraced electric furnaces and automation. Can the reader think of similar cases?

George Orwell's observations on conformism are frightening, but correspond well with my own experiences. As you read the following excerpts from Nineteen Eighty-four, mentally replace Orwell's "the Party" with "the Corporation's top management."

"... The essence of oligarchical rule is not father-to-son inheritance, but the persistence of a certain world-view and a certain way of life ... A ruling group is a ruling group so long as it can nominate its successors. The Party is not concerned with perpetuating its blood but with perpetuating itself. Who wields power is not important, provided that the hierarchical structure remains always the same ... What opinions the masses hold, or do not hold, is looked on as a matter of indifference. In a Party member, on the other hand, not even the smallest deviation of opinion on the most unimportant subject can be tolerated. ... On the other hand, his actions are not regulated by law or by any clearly formulated code of behavior. ... A Party member is required to have not only the right opinions, but the right instincts. Many of the beliefs and attitudes demanded of him are never plainly stated, and could not be stated without laying bare the contradiction [in the system]. ... [His characteristics] include the power of not grasping analogies, of failing to perceive logical errors, of misunderstanding the simplest arguments if they are inimical to [the system], and of being bored or repelled by any train of thought which is capable of leading in a heretical direction.

"... Doublethink means the power of holding two contradictory beliefs in one's mind simultaneously, and accepting both of them. ... The essential act of the Party is to use conscious deception while retaining the firmness of purpose that goes with complete honesty. To tell deliberate lies while genuinely believing in them, to forget any fact that has become inconvenient, and then, when it becomes necessary again, to draw it back from oblivion for just so long as it is needed, to deny the existence of objective reality and all the while to take account of the reality which one denied - all this is indispensably necessary. ... For the secret of rulership is to combine a belief in one's own infallibility with the power to learn from past mistakes. ... For it is only by reconciling contradictions that power can be retained indefinitely.

"... What was required in a Party member was an outlook similar to that of the ancient Hebrew who knew, without knowing much else, that all nations other than his own worshipped 'false gods.' ... The Party member knew what constituted right conduct, and in exceedingly vague, generalized terms he knew what kinds of departure from it were possible.

"... Only the disciplined mind can see reality. You believe that reality is something objective, external, existing in its own right. ... But I tell you that reality is not external. Reality exists in the human mind and nowhere else. Not in the individual mind, which can make mistakes, and in any case soon perishes; only in the mind of the Party, which is collective and immortal. Whatever the Party holds to be truth is truth. It is impossible to see reality except by looking through the eyes of the Party."

I will never forget the day a top manager - let's call him "Volpone" - told me: "You are out of touch with reality," after I had tried to explain to him, figures in hand, that Project X, supposedly a cost-savings measure, was actually going to waste money. Never mind that all the other technically knowledgeable middle-managers shared my views. What counted was that there were strong non-economic organizational reasons to pursue Project X, but Volpone had to provide an economic justification. So, in his reality, which was the reality of the corporation, Project X would save costs. Volpone was a master at corporate doublethink and I learned much from him, albeit painfully.

What I learned was double-edged: on one side, how to survive in that particular oligarchic organization; on the other side, what is wrong with a clubby oligarchy.

Machiavelli again:

A boss can never assure himself against the hostility of all the employees, because they are too many; he can assure himself against other managers, because they are few. The worst a boss can expect from the enmity of all the employees is to be abandoned; but from managers who are enemies, he must fear not just being abandoned, but also that they will move against him; because, since managers are more astute, and know more, they always have time to protect their own interest, and to seek favour with whomever they expect to win.

It is necessary for the boss to retain the majority of the employees, but he can at any time get rid of the other managers, and replace them as he wishes. (IX-3)

In other words, the employees as a whole can only go on strike or engage in slowdowns, whereas subordinate management can conspire with higher management to replace the boss. Strikes can be unpredictable and unavoidable (although enlightened labor relations reduce their likelihood), whereas an astute boss should be able to avoid conspiracies among his subordinates. The boss cannot fire the entire workforce, he can only fire his subordinates.

Can the reader think of cases where a boss has been unseated by a conspiracy of his subordinates? Can you think of cases where top management and the board of directors have conspired to replace a chief executive?

I have never seen a manager demoted because he was unpopular with his employees. Such cases are rare. One occurred when a school board sacked the superintendent after concluding that he had provoked a needless teachers' strike. More common is a subordinate's cabal which can either reduce the effectiveness of a hated superior, or result in him being viewed in a bad light by upper management. For instance, I heard of a hospital food-service department where the manager was fired when the assistant manager and the dietician conspired with the head nurse to convince top brass that the manager was inattentive to patients' needs. A subsequent investigation cleared the food-service manager- but too late to help him..

As Machiavelli says:

And, to clarify this subject further, I will explain how subordinate managers must be considered in two ways. Either they act in such a way that they become entirely dependent on your fortune, or not: those that do, and are not greedy, must be honored and loved.

Those who hold back, fall into two categories. Some fail to commit themselves because of cowardice and lack of spirit; then you should make use of those that are experts in some area, since they will honor you in prosperity, and you need not fear them in adversity. But, if they deliberately refrain from

*becoming loyal to you because of their own
ambition, it is a sign that they think more of
themselves than of you; and you, the boss, must
always watch such people, and fear them as if
they were open enemies, because, in adversity,
they will always help to ruin you. (IX-4)*

Has the reader has experience with any of the types of
subordinates that Machiavelli describes here? Have you been
one of those types?

*In my own career, many years ago, I incurred the
displeasure of a superior because I made clear
that I was not dependent on him, and showed
that I was thinking more of my career than of
his.*

*Over the years, I have found that promotion
comes faster if you show that you completely
support your boss, and are dependent on him.
At the lower levels of management,
Machiavelli's other approach also works well:
you show that you are an expert in your field,
with no ambitions to move too high.*

As Machiavelli put it:

*Someone who becomes boss against the will of
the employees, but with the favour of other
managers, must above all other things win the
favour of the employees: this is easy if he
undertakes to protect them. Because people,*

when they are well treated by someone from whom they expected injury, become even more dependent on their benefactor than if they had chosen him themselves. (IX-5)

Can you think of any manager who has been successful without motivating the majority of his employees?

Machiavelli's maxim applies to the letter to something that happened to me. I was promoted to be head of a department by local geographical management, against the wishes of headquarters functional management (it was a matrix-managed organization). Functional management did its best to convince the local employees that I would be a disaster as manager. Once I took over, I improved their working situation, so that they quickly became totally loyal to me, going out of their way to defend me against functional management at headquarters.

Machiavelli again:

I will conclude by saying that it is necessary for a boss to have all employees on his side, otherwise he has no remedy to adversity. ... If a boss has confidence in employees as a whole, is able to lead and has guts, is not paralyzed by adversity, is not deficient in planning, is able to motivate by example and by leading, then he

> *will never be deceived by his employees, and he will see that he has laid a good foundation. (IX-6)*

Can you think of a manager that was bailed out of a tough spot by an extra effort on the part of his department as a whole? Can you think of a successful boss without this kind of loyalty?

> *Most of us have experienced such loyalty on both sides: as followers and as leaders. When there is a "good foundation," as Machiavelli says, children make extra efforts for parents, teams for coaches, soldiers for generals, and employees for bosses.*

Machiavelli again:

> *A boss leads either directly, or through his subordinate managers. In the second case his power is weaker and less secure, because it depends on the will of his subordinates, who, especially during times of adversity, can remove him from power, either by acting against him or by not obeying him.*
>
> *In an adversity, the boss does not have time to assert his direct leadership, because the employees, who are used to obeying the other managers, are not, in the circumstances, ready to obey him directly; so, during hard times, he will always lack people whom he can trust. Such*

> a boss cannot base himself on what he sees
> when all is well and all employees need their
> jobs, because all profess their loyalty when
> adversity is hidden; but, when adversity is
> present, when the organization needs its
> employees, then one finds few to count on.
>
> Therefore a wise boss must always think of a
> way to make sure that all the employees, always
> and in all circumstance, need him and their jobs
> in the organization: then they will always be
> faithful. (IX-7)

In most business organizations, managers cannot lead directly, but must do so through subordinate managers. What steps do effective managers take in order to assure the loyalty of employees? How about mixing with employees, informal discussions with employees, quality circles? Can you think of companies that try to assure employee loyalty by higher-than-average benefits or salaries or promises of job security or opportunities for promotion? Are these measures effective?

> One high-level manager I knew, and the one I
> still respect most as a practitioner of
> Machiavelli's maxims, had the unconventional
> habit of getting deeply involved in all the hiring,
> promotion, and salary-increase decisions of his
> subordinate managers. Thus he broke one of the
> textbook rules about delegation of authority.
> Usually his involvement was so subtle that his

subordinates were unaware of it. Moreover, most of his deputies knew that they owed their jobs to him; as for the few who resisted, he risked offending them, while being wary of hostile conspiracies.

Since everyone in the department know who made the real hiring and promotion decisions, all departmental employees knew to whom they really owed loyalty, so the high-level manager knew that he could always trust all his people, when the going was tough.

The classic way for a boss to exert leadership over all followers, no matter how far-flung or subdivided is twofold: results plus reminders. During World War II, Patton's men - regardless of regiment or division - were constantly reminded that they belonged to Patton's Third Army and that it got results. At Ford Motor Company, when it still commanded 59% of the US automobile market in the 1920s, the original Henry Ford never let his thousands of employees forget that his genius produced this result.[12]

---

[12] The book GM Passes Ford by Arthur J. Kuhn (Penn State, 1986), shows how Ford's market share dropped from 59% to 10% while GM's rose from 15% to 40%. Ford's decline resulted from the founder's failure to obey two of Machiavelli's precepts: early recognition of problems (Chapter 11) and continual improvement to meet competition (Chapter 23). The present Ford management has done much to regain the company's competitive edge.

8. How to Rate the Ability of Bosses to Stay in Power

We should examine whether a boss has enough power so that he can maintain his position by himself, or whether he always needs help from others.

In the second case one can say nothing except to counsel the boss to protect his territory, and to ignore other departments. And whoever has protected his territory well, and has managed his department according to what was said above and according to what will be said below, will only be attacked with great respect; because people are always inimical to ventures that appear difficult, nor can it appear easy to attack someone who has protected his turf and is not hated by his employees. (X-1)

Here Machiavelli makes the point, often overlooked, that your job security depends not merely on the strength of your positions but also on the strength of your boss's position. If your boss is the owner and is threatened by bankruptcy or a hostile takeover, the point is obvious. But suppose your boss is a corporate executive and has a weak position in the company. I know of two cases where very capable employees suffered from the bosses' vulnerability.

One case was in a publishing company, where several highly-skilled editors became "orphans" when the head of their division was moved into a meaningless staff job (a "special project"). This division head was a respected former editor, but he had failed to protect his flanks, so his division was absorbed little by little by more aggressive divisions. Moreover, his editors had failed to assist their boss in defending his turf.

In another case, in a plant that manu-factured airframes, the head of the mold loft (let's call him "Icarus") was terminated on the ground that he had no future with the corporation. Icarus was highly capable and well-liked by his engineering staff, but he was a loner who had failed to participate in corporate activities, whether professional or social. Since Icarus was clearly incapable of protecting his position, his staff faced an unwelcome choice when they saw him fall from favor: whether to try to replace Icarus or to seek greener pastures in a different company.

Can you think of an otherwise strong manager who has failed to guard his turf? Conversely, can you think of a weak manager who has built barriers around his department and who protects his territory? Would it be easy to attack such a manager?

I have seen more examples than I can count. In one spectacular case, even top management was afraid to take on the manager in question. Despite the fact that the department performed an obscure technical function, its manager had created such a mystique about it that no one dared to take the risk of meddling with it. That was so even though the department was managed in such a way as to contribute as little as possible to the company as a whole.

Machiavelli again:

A strong and courageous boss can sustain even a determined attack against his territory, by assuring his employees that the worst will not last long, by creating fear for the cruelty of the enemy, and by using skill to restrain those that seem too audacious. ... The nature of people is to feel as obligated for services which they give as for services which they receive. (X-3)

Did you ever observe some remote operation come under pressure from corporate headquarters to reduce expenses or whatever? Did corporate headquarters win? Did local management use any of the techniques mentioned above?

I know of a New York corporation in which the Southeastern (Atlanta) sales office was closed after top management questioned its value and its staff fell apart, from the boss down to the file clerk. By contrast, the staff of the West Coast (San Francisco) sales office closed ranks when threatened, and went on to prove its value. The different outcomes reflected the different leadership styles of the two regional sales managers: that is, the bosses.

Dramatic examples occur during mergers and takeovers. I was deeply involved in one case where my company (let's call it "Goliath Inc.") was taking over a former competitor ("David Inc."). In David we confronted a number of strong department managers who threatened to mobilize resistance against a smooth takeover. Since we at Goliath recognized this threat early, we moved energetically to convince the David bosses and their subordinates that there were promising jobs for them at Goliath and that they would actually be better off with us. Our tactics worked. Most of the David bosses transferred their loyalty to Goliath, while the few hold-outs became isolated and resigned. At Goliath we recognized Machiavelli's advice about bosses' protective attitudes toward their turf, and used it in our favor.

9. On Bureaucracies

In bureaucracies one becomes a boss either through skill or through luck, and maintains power without either skill or luck; because bureaucracies are governed by ancient ways of doing things, which are so strong and of such a nature, that bosses remain in power no matter what they do and no matter how they act.

Only these people have authority that cannot be taken away from them; employees that are not managed; departments that, while not managed, are not taken away from them; and the employees, while they are not managed, do not care, nor do they think, nor can they become alienated from their bosses.

Therefore these are the only organizations that enjoy security and happiness. (XI-1)

Machiavelli speaks of states governed by ecclesiastical rulers, which I have translated as bureaucracies, since many Roman Catholic bishops (and the Pope), during the Renaissance, ruled as princes with bureaucratic organizations. His reference to "happiness" is ironic, as in the old schoolteacher's challenge: "Would you rather be a happy pig or an unhappy Socrates?"

The reader might find some similarities to modern bureaucracies, governmental or corporate.

To my knowledge few corporate bureaucracies attain the sublime level of detachment from reality and contempt for the public (including customers) that Machiavelli speaks of (but there are some that do). Consider the case of a prominent mail-order house. For years it sold an item called "Western riding boots." Then it added an item by a well-known designer under the heading "Weston riding boots." Many customers who ordered the new item received good old Western riding boots. When the sales manager complained to the warehouse manager, this corporate bureaucrat told him that such an error was impossible because his staff (pickers and packers) used stock numbers exclusively and paid no attention to item names. When the sales manager asked the bureaucrat how he knew that his staff relied on stock numbers, he was told: "Because I gave them written instructions to do so, and they all initialled my memo - even the union shop steward." The evidence of the mistaken shipments did not count! In the mind of a true bureaucrat, procedural reality outweighs factual reality.

On the other hand, I know of many, many governmental bureaucracies to which

Machiavelli's words apply. Consider the three excuses of the civil servants of a particularly ancient and well-entrenched European bureaucracy. These are responses to a proposal for a new way of doing something:

1) We always do it this way.

2) We have never done it that way.

3) If we did it that way, everyone would want it (and we would be overwhelmed).

10. On the Importance of Sales People

> *We have said above, that a boss must have a good foundation, otherwise he will of necessity come to ruin.*
>
> *The main foundations that all companies must have are a good organization and good sales people. And since there cannot be a good organization where there are not good sales people ... I will leave organization aside and speak of sales. (XII-1)*

Machiavelli speaks of laws and armies. I have translated this as organization and sales people, since, just as armies are essential for maintaining the integrity of a state, so are sales people essential for ensuring the continued existence of a company. If you are in business, does your company recognize the importance of sales personnel? What other human factors are essential to the continued existence of a business organization?

> *By definition, a commercial company must sell to survive. It is an axiom of capitalism that the older the industry, the keener the competition. Thus the importance of selling keeps growing as the market grows. Occasionally a company introduces a product with so spontaneous a*

---

[13] See GM Passes Ford: 1918-1938, by Arthur J. Kuhn (Penn State Press, 1986)

demand that the product almost sells itself. Even in such situations, however, after the start-up phase, selling becomes essential. (When I speak of selling, I refer to the whole process of marketing - from research to advertising - as well as the vital role of sales people.)

Consider the case of Ford Motor Company and the General Motors Corporation (GM) in the early days of the automobile. From Ford's founding in 1903 until 1921, its market share climbed to 59%, quite an achievement in manufacturing. Ford's plain black Model T provided cheap, dependable transportation and practically sold itself. But, in the 1930s, GM began to sell varied styles and colors, with the result that its share rose to above 40% while Ford's fell to about 15%. Neither initial advantage or manufacturing know-how, both possessed by Ford, could overcome the lack of a good marketing and sales team.[13]

No clever organization, no amount of management science, no hordes of MBA's, can overcome a lack of good sales and marketing. I have seen competitors of companies that I worked for fail, when they ignored this fundamental fact of life.

As Machiavelli puts it:

I say, therefore, that the sales team on whom a boss relies for the continued existence of his company is either his own or external distributors.

Distributors are useless and dangerous, and, if your sales are based on external distributors, your organization will never be stable nor secure; because they are divided, ambitious, undisciplined, unfaithful, courageous when among friends, cowardly when confronted by enemies ... when there is no competition you are despoiled by them, when there is competition you are despoiled by your competitors.

The reason is that distributors have no other love, nor any other reason to be on your side, than a little bit of money, which is not enough to assure their loyalty. They like to be on your side so long as there is no competition, but as soon as things are difficult, they run away or leave you. (XII-2)

Machiavelli speaks of mercenary armies, which I have translated as distributors. Readers who have worked in organizations that relied excessively on distributors for sales might be able to see some similarities between what Machiavelli says and modern business.

I have worked in a company where we had no choice but to sell through distributors. So long

> as we had the best product, they were beating on our doors. When competitors arrived, they started to demand bigger and bigger discounts; they threatened to start distributing the competitor's products; they forced us to do work that they should have been doing; and so forth.
>
> As Machiavelli says, a little bit of money (in the form of a distributor discount) does not buy much loyalty, and it buys you no control.

The same maxim might also apply to any use of outside consultants or outside service organizations for services that are essential for the survival of the company.

> But I have worked in an organization that was very successful in subcontracting all work that was not essential for survival. This organization took to heart one of Peter Drucker's recommendations, and focused its resources on its mission. All ancillary functions were subcontracted.

11. What a Boss Must Do: Six Rules for Success

The boss who does not recognize problems when they arise is not really wise; but such wisdom is given to few. (XIII-7)

I have known only one person who had that wisdom, and he spent an inordinate amount of time and energy in looking over the horizon for problems that might come up.

In contrast, consider Sears-Roebuck, which has fallen from its position as the world's number one retailer. Because its top management was slow to recognize the company's problems, Sears was forced into a drastic reorganization in 1993. That reorganization included dropping its century-old mail-order catalog, the world's first. Sears' top management had failed to recognize a two-fold change in consumer preference: first, toward specialty mail-order houses like L. L. Bean or Colonial Garden Kitchen; second, toward quick-service drive-up stores exemplified by K-Mart and Wal-Mart. Can you think of other cases of blindness to problems until the "eleventh hour"?

As Machiavelli says:

A boss therefore must have no other objective, nor thought, nor learn any other skill, aside from the primary purpose of the organization for which he is responsible, because this is the only skill that is required of the leader.

This is so important, that not only does it maintain bosses in power, but it often results in ordinary employees becoming bosses; and on the contrary one sees that, when bosses have thought more about nonessential things than about their primary purpose, they have lost their jobs.

And the main reason for losing your job is to neglect your primary purpose; and the main reason for being promoted is to be an expert in the primary purpose of your job. (XIV-1)

Machiavelli speaks of the necessity for the prince to be an expert in the art of war, which, as he reiterates, is the activity that is essential for the survival of a state. In order to facilitate broader application of Machiavelli's observations, I have translated "art of war" as primary "purpose of an organization."

Since selling is essential to a company's survival, it is often regarded as its primary purpose, often rightly but sometimes wrongly. Savings and loan associations, for example, went astray when salesmen took precedence over loan officers. On the other hand, the US automobile industry lost market share to Japanese manufacturers by neglecting market research, a sales function. A logician looking at business would describe the role of selling as necessary but not sufficient. Within companies, departments have different primary purposes. As a consequence, the importance of individual skills varies correspondingly. For example, real-time inventory control requires mastery of real-time software. The impact of such a control system on the purchasing, transportation, and warehousing functions is obvious.

Can you think of anyone who was promoted because he or she was an expert at a job considered essential to the department? How about someone who was demoted because, as a result of technological change or some other change in circumstances, he or she no longer had a skill considered essential?

> *I have never known anyone to be promoted from rank-and-file employee to first-line supervisor unless he or she was one of the most skilled employees in the department, with regard to an essential function.*
>
> *And I have seen, more than once, department managers lose their jobs when they have been unable to maintain technical expertise in rapidly evolving areas that were essential for the operation of their department.*

Machiavelli indulges in a bit of hyperbole when he implies that only one essential skill is needed for success. Of course other skills - for example basic management skills - are needed to be successful. Some of these other skills have already been mentioned, and others will be mentioned later in this book.

There is no comparison between someone who has expert skills and someone who does not; and it is not reasonable that someone who is knowledgeable should willingly obey someone who is not, and that the ignorant should remain safely surrounded by experts.

Furthermore, since the expert is full of indignation, and the ignoramus full of suspicion, it is not possible for them to work well together. Therefore, a boss that does not understand the work of his department cannot, aside from all else, be respected by his employees, nor have faith in them. (XIV-2)

Here Machiavelli contradicts the widespread modern notion that a good manager can manage anything. Does Machiavelli's observation match your experience? Did you ever know a manager who failed because he understood nothing of the work that his or her department was supposed to do? Did you ever observe a good manager quickly learn enough about a new department to be able to help his or her employees to do a better job?

In my experience, while successful managers must have basic management skills, their prime qualification is to know enough about the business at hand to be able to make the tough decisions that ensure survival.

Look at the recent troubles in the computer industry: most of the companies that have failed, have been acquired, or are in deep trouble are those whose top management is heavy with non-experts such as accountants. The companies that are surviving - or better yet, prospering - are those managed at the top by people who know how to build and sell computers.

Machiavelli again:

And I have never met a successful first- or middle-level manager who was not an expert in the field of activity of his or her department. He or she might not have been an expert when promoted, but quickly put considerable energy into becoming an expert. The boss must, therefore, never take his thoughts away from the purpose of his organization ... (XIV-3)

All of the successful managers that I know focus fiercely on the real missions of their departments (which might differ somewhat from the "official mission" described on paper). A friend of mine in the school textbook business received a directive to "increase market share." She translated this to mean "keep our textbooks in line with changes in school curriculums." When a newspaper publisher was instructed to "cut printing costs," he knew this meant "learn about computer technology applied to printing."

As Machiavelli put it:

Often a great leader asked questions of this nature: suppose the competition took such an action, and we reacted thusly, which of us would have the advantage? How could we reorganize to meet their threat? ... And he proposed for discussion all situations that could arise; he listened to the opinions of his colleagues, then stated his own, and the reasons behind it: so that thanks to these continual thoughts there never arose a situation that he was not prepared to handle. (XIV-4)

But, in what concerns exercising the mind, the boss must read case histories, and in these consider the actions of excellent leaders to see how they managed, to examine the reasons for their successes and failures, in order to be able to avoid failure and attain success. (XIV-5)

Do you follow Machiavelli's advice? Specifically, do you read and discuss case histories in business newspapers, magazines, and books, in order to help to understand what other managers do right and wrong?

A wealth of business case histories are readily available. For instance, I have under my eyes six randomly selected copies of The Wall Street Journal, for six different days. There are three front-page stories each day, for a total of 18 stories. Of the 18 stories, 8 are analyses or case histories related to mainstream businesses, 5 are related to politics or political leaders, 3 are analyses or case histories of unusual businesses, 2 are human interest stories. Thus 60% of the stories are intended to help managers learn from the experiences of other managers.

A more detailed analysis of the contents of the Journal, or of such publications as Business Week, The Economist, Forbes, Fortune, Management International would confirm that case histories form an important part of the appeal of these publications. The same is true of books and journals directed to particular industries or to particular functions (from accounting to warehousing).

Machiavelli again:

A wise boss must never stay idle during good times, but must work hard to capitalize on them, in order to be able to profit from them in adversity, so that, when fortune changes, he will be able to resist the change. (XIV-5)

Here Machiavelli is making the often-neglected point that we can learn from successes as well as failures. When things go right, we can analyze why and how, in order to be better prepared when things start to go wrong. Does your company or department follow this practice? Can you use your influence to get it going?

> *In most of the organizations that I have worked for, there has been a highly visible bulletin board or newsletter, where we could publish charts or stories illustrating recent successes in our department or in the company.*

12. On Those Actions for Which People, Especially Bosses, are Praised or Blamed

Many have imagined organizations that have never been seen nor known to exist in reality.

Since we live so differently from the way we should live, whoever ignores what is done, in favour of what should be done, learns how to ruin himself rather than how to survive: because a person who wishes to be virtuous in all things must come to ruin when surrounded by so many who are not virtuous.

Hence it is necessary for a boss, if he wishes to maintain power, to learn how to be not virtuous, and to use or not use this ability according to necessity. (XV-1)

We see clearly here what I call Machiavelli's "scientific cynicism". I use the word cynicism in its original sense of this-wordly practicality, as opposed to other-worldly utopianism. Machiavelli observes that we do not live in the ideal, perfect world that we would like to live in, and that, in order to survive in this imperfect world, we must act in ways that would not be needed in those ideal, perfect worlds that we can imagine, but that do not exist.

Does it ever seem to you that, at times, persons in higher levels of management appear to violate basic principles of conduct? Think about national leaders; generals or admirals;

captains of industry; and your own bosses. What principles do they sometimes seem to violate? If we apply Machiavelli's this-wordly standards to their behavior, can we understand and accept it?

One example comes to mind from my experience. Many years ago, I worked for a corporation in which top management undertook a reorganization involving the shutdown of a production unit. Rumors were flying about possible layoffs, and the concerned employees were worried. Since we needed their contribution until the last minute, their boss stood up in front of them, denied the rumors, and promised that their jobs were safe. Six months later, they were all offered a severance package.

Unethical? Well, at first I was shocked, but later I put the events into perspective. First of all, the closure was necessary from a business point of view. Furthermore, the manager in question needed to hold the organization together during the six-month period of reorganization. Technically, the manager did not lie, since he never said how long the threatened jobs would be safe. This point may seem to be a mere "technicality," but nearly all bosses must use such devices as a last resort.

Machiavelli again:

I know that everyone will agree that it would be very praiseworthy if a boss had all the qualities that are held to be good; but, since he cannot have them all, nor always practice them because the human condition does not permit doing so, the boss must be prudent enough to avoid completely those flaws that would cost him his job, and, if possible, to eschew those that would not cost him his job; but, if avoiding the latter is not possible, he can indulge in these flaws with less circumspection. (XV-3)

One of the greatest military and political leaders of all time, Temuchin, Genghis Khan (1162-1227), put the matter in the following way: "It would be seemly to get drunk only three times a month. It would be preferable, clearly, to make it only twice or even only once. It would be perfect never to get drunk at all. But where is the man who could observe such a rule of conduct?"

Have you ever had a boss with no personal bad habits? If so, he or she must have been an insufferable prig. The important question, for a boss or anyone else, is whether behavioral flaws detract from performance. Can you think of cases where personal flaws have, or have not, detracted from a boss's performance?

The definition of personal misbehavior varies from time to time and place to place. What is considered acceptable tipsiness in one place is seen as intolerable drunkenness in another. Any use of alcohol, or even tobacco, is viewed as a vice, if not a sin, in some social environments. Innocent cussing in one place would be forbidden profanity in another. Football pools would be sinful gambling to some bosses. Behavior that may have been treated as acceptable flirting at one time is now widely regarded as sexual harassment. There is also the question of the extent to which an employer has the right to consider an employee's behavior outside the workplace. No employer wants to have the "town drunk" or "skirt chaser" or the payroll, but should an otherwise satisfactory employee be fired (or even disadvantaged) because he or she has a reputation as an after-hours "barfly," "womanizer," or "pushover"? Every boss or would-be boss should establish a set of standards by which to test his own personal behavior and that of his subordinates and superiors. Such standards should include tolerance of minor slips, since few mortals are perfect - and those few are certainly not in business.

> *And furthermore the boss should not care if he incurs blame from questionable behavior without which he would have difficulty in preserving his organization; because, if we consider all things thoroughly, we will find some things that seem virtuous but would result in ruin, and others that seem not virtuous but would result in security and well-being. (XV-3)*

Here Machiavelli looks at another side of a boss's need to follow this-worldly practicality rather than other-worldly utopianism: public blame. Early in this chapter we considered the case of a boss who laid off employees after seeming to promise job security. He took a roasting from those who knew the events - even though the action was necessary. Public blame is part of the price of accepting authority. As President Harry Truman put the matter: "If you can't stand the heat, stay out of the kitchen." Have you seen cases where a boss had to take "the heat" for a necessary action?

> Public blame can be especially hot when a founder is forced out. We all know such cases. I know a case of a floor-covering firm. The founder was brilliant at both buying and selling. He purchased the best tiles, carpeting, and adhesives at favorable prices, and he merchandised them so that his floors became legendary. But "Mr. Floor's" entrepreneurial genius got out of hand, as often happens, and turned into incurable over-expansion. He opened too many branches and added too many sidelines such as wall-coverings. Finally his financial backers forced him to step aside into a consulting role, and to accept a skilled manager as the boss. Would you be willing and able to take the heat which that new boss felt?

13. On Being Generous or Parsimonious

A boss who cannot be generous without damage to his organization, must not, if he is wise, care whether he is called a miser: because with time he will be held generous, once it is seen that his budget is balanced thanks to his parsimony. (XVI-2)

When cost reductions are necessary, they must be undertaken no matter how unpleasant. When we judge cost reductions, especially as they affect us, our honesty is put on trial. Can you think of cases where cost reductions resulted in an ultimate strengthening of the organization, and in praise for the cost cutters? Be honest!

I have gone through cost reductions more times than I can remember. Everybody (including me) always complains when the budget-cutting knife is sharpened. Our complaints are always the same: the cuts are too large and unfairly distributed. Each time, everyone knows that the cost cutters have gone too far: that essential operations will be unfavorably affected; that no more cuts are possible.

Some time later, when we look back, we see that the organization was actually improved: the cuts forced us to focus on essential operations, and to stop doing things that contributed little to the true mission of the organization. The boss who ordered the cuts soars from miser to savior.

14. On Whether it is Better to be Loved than Feared or Better to be Feared than Loved

> *Every boss must wish to be considered nice and not tough: however, he must be careful not to misuse his niceness.*
>
> *A boss must not mind whether he is considered tough when he takes actions to keep his employees working well: since, if he takes a few tough actions, he will actually be nicer than those who, by acting too nice, let discipline deteriorate.*
>
> *That is so because a general deterioration offends all employees, while a few tough actions offend only those concerned.*
>
> *... Nevertheless, the boss must judge and take action slowly and deliberately, must not scare himself, and must proceed with prudence and humanity, avoiding recklessness due to overconfidence and intolerance due to suspicion.*
> *(XVII-1)*

Have you ever known a department where efficiency suffered because the boss was too nice? Did some employees take advantage of the boss's niceness? Did the department's morale suffer for that reason?

We have all seen cases where some employees are allowed to break rules, such as rules about working hours, because the boss is trying to be nice about these employees' personal problems. The result is a drop in overall discipline - as well as morale - because a workplace is not a psychiatric hospital. If the boss takes tough action against the rule-breakers, they may complain, but the rest of the department will applaud (sometimes silently). Excessive delegation is another example of over-niceness.

All subordinates are flattered when a manager gives them greater authority; yet the boss errs when he gives a subordinate more power than he or she can handle. A boss also errs when he does not give the subordinate adequate guidance, but, in an effort to be liked, continually refers matters for decision back to the subordinate, by saying: "How do you think we should handle it?"

Although General McClellan defeated General Lee at Antietam, President Lincoln removed the victorious general from command because his victory was not decisive. One reason the outcome was not decisive was that McClellan had delegated too much authority to one of his corps commanders: he was being nice to a friend. The friend failed to follow the battle plan, reducing the scope of the victory.

Linda A. Hill of the Harvard Business School describes the traits that a new boss must cultivate: "They must learn to lead rather than do, to win trust and respect, to motivate both the individual and the group, and to strike a balance between delegation and control."[14] Note that "being liked" is not mentioned.

Control through firm leadership, to use Prof. Hill's words, is what Machiavelli urges. And he warns against "recklessness due to over-confidence and intolerance due to suspicion." Have you ever observed excessive toughness resulting from this pair of unhealthy traits?

> *An example of excessive toughness born of haste, arrogance and overconfidence. A young manager was moving very quickly up the ranks of the organization. When he reached the lowest level of the top-management layer he started to throw his weight around without mercy. Anyone on his path had to change priorities, or work overtime, in order to meet his requirements, at once, or else. A quote: "Do you know who I am and how much power I have around here?" Was he successful? No, he changed companies.*
>
> *The other extreme: someone I know well, who has three good traits: he is nice, nice and nice. You will not be surprised to learn that he did not remain a manager for a very long time. He was unable to prevent the inevitable bad apple from ruining the efficiency of his department.*

---

[14] From Becoming a Manager: Mastery of a New Identity by Linda A. Hill (Boston, 1992)

As Machiavelli says:

The foregoing rule gives rise to the question: is it better to be loved than feared, or better to be feared than loved?

The answer is that we wish to be both; but, since it is difficult to be both, it is much safer to be feared rather than loved, if we must forgo one of the two.

That is so because of people one can say this in general: that they are ungrateful, fickle, deceitful, and dissembling; avoiders of danger; and greedy. As long as you do something for them, they are all yours so long as adversity is far away; but when adversity comes, they rebel.

People hesitate less to offend someone who has made himself loved than someone who has made himself feared; because love is maintained by a tie which people, since people are bad, they will easily break for the sake of self-interest; whereas fear is maintained by the dread of punishment, and this is always present. (XVII-2)

There is another of Machiavelli's "scientifically cynical" judgements. It is scientific in the sense that it is based on observation. It is cynical because Machiavelli's outlook was pessimistic. Almost two centuries later the French moralist La Bruyère reached the same conclusion: "Let us not feel animadversion against mankind when we see hardened hearts, ingratitude, injustice, pride, love of oneself and thoughtlessness towards others; such are men, it is their nature: it would be like not being able to bear that stones fall or that fire rises."

A less pessimistic observer might conclude that some, even most, mortals are not so contemptible. Yet even the most optimistic observer must admit that many humans have weak natures. That being so, a prudent boss will use fear - the threat of punishment - to keep his weaker subordinates in line.

> *One of the most effective managers I have ever known, a man who was not particularly brilliant in any way, deliberately used fear in order to enforce respect for his views and decisions. He made clear to his subordinates that he would not hesitate to use his managerial power against them, if they crossed him. Since he did not flaunt his power, or use it capriciously, he did not offend his stronger subordinates. The weaker ones, moreover, viewed him with respect rather than hatred. The line between fear plus respect, on the one hand, and offensiveness plus hatred, on the other hand, is thin. It is difficult to steer a course between the two without error.*
>
> *Easily the worst manager I have ever had the misfortune to work with - let's call him "Boney"*

- was one who incurred contempt and hatred because he appeared to use his power arbitrarily, with no regard for the opinions of any of his subordinates. In fact, he had been given ambitious objectives by higher management; achieving them required the adroit use of power, because significant change in the department's working methods was required (refer back to Chapter 4 for Machiavelli's views on how to manage change).

Unfortunately, Boney was one of those people who want to be liked by everyone and who avoid any form of inter-personal conflict as if it were the plague. In order to avoid challenges to his decisions, he avoided making them public until the last possible moment. Then he sprung them on people by surprise. The result? Resistance to change was far greater than it would have been if people had felt somehow involved in the decision-making process. Boney clearly thought that being perceived as "nice" was more important than being perceived as "tough". But the department's objectives forced him to be tough, and his attempts to project an image of "niceness" only succeeded in brewing tremendous insecurity and resentment in the

94

> *department: people were literally spending hours a week trying to figure out what the "secret plans" were that the boss was hiding from them.*

Machiavelli again:

> *Nevertheless, the boss must make himself feared in such a way that, if he does not gain love, he avoids hatred. Indeed he can easily be feared and not hated; and he will achieve this standing so long as he avoids offending his employees. (XVII-3)*

To summarize Machiavelli's advice, we can say that a boss who is feared and not hated is respected, and that it is better to be respected than to be loved. Can you think of some truly outstanding managers that you know? Are they both loved and respected? Can you think of managers who are more loved than respected? Have they been effective in both easy and tough times?

> *I once knew a very effective and successful manager who was both loved and respected. He was promoted, and continued to act as he had in the past. But the new environment was tougher, more competitive, and he failed, because he put more emphasis on being loved than on being feared. When I last knew him, he was outside the chain of command, in the harmless role of "Special Projects Manager".*

15. On the Way Bosses Should Keep Faith: the Limits of Candor

Everyone knows how praiseworthy it is for a boss to keep his word and to rely on honesty rather than cunning.

Nevertheless we see from experience that in our times those bosses who have achieved great things have put little stock in integrity, and that they have used cunning to manipulate the minds of people; and in the end they have surpassed those who relied on honesty. (XVIII-1)

This famous chapter is often cited to show Machiavelli's "utter cynicism." Note, however, that he is reporting his honest conclusions from careful observation of human behavior: in other words, a "scientific cynicism." Not also that Machiavelli accepted the Judeo-Christian view of humans as inherently sinful (or fallible), a view shared by many other great thinkers.

I shall never forget one example of "creative cunning" that would have flunked the test of honesty. A division manager - let's call him "Conn" - showed a sales forecast projecting a steady increase, reversing a steady decline to date. When questioned by his superiors and peers, he explained that many factors had changed, though he was vague about them.

Sales continued to decline for several months while Conn stuck to his optimistic forecasts and vague explanations. Finally sales improved, thanks partly to improved conditions and partly to Conn's actions.

If Conn had been honest at the beginning, he would not have had the chance to take action to correct the problems: his superiors and peers would not have had confidence in him.

Machiavelli again:

Therefore you must know that there are two ways to fight: the first relying on laws, the second relying on force. The first is characteristic of people, the second of animals. But as the first is often not enough, one must sometimes rely on the second. (XVIII-2)

Although Machiavelli prefers a civilized rule of law, he recognizes that a resort to force is sometimes necessary, because of what John Adams later called "the lust of mankind after dominion." This is why states have armies and police forces and why businesses have security departments. Occasionally even managerial personnel must be restrained or expelled by force. Do you know of such cases?

I have experienced several. In once case a department manager abused his authority to monitor phone calls and was systematically recording the conversations of his direct superior. When confronted, he had the effrontery to deny the facts! In another case, an employee was occasionally suspending his work for 15-30 minutes in order to commit adultery, on company premises, with another employee.

As Machiavelli says:

The boss must be able to use the skills of the fox and the lion; because a lion cannot avoid a trap, and a fox cannot defend itself from wolves. He must therefore be a fox in order to recognize traps, and a lion in order to scare away wolves. Those who try to live like the lion alone are seriously mistaken.

Therefore a wise boss cannot, and should not, keep his word when doing so would injure him and when the reasons that made him promise good faith are no longer there.

If people were all good, this maxim would not be good; but since people are bad, and will not keep faith with you, you need not keep faith with them. Nor will the boss ever lack legitimate reasons for explaining lack of faith.

He that has best used the nature of the fox has had the most success. But it is necessary to know how to misrepresent well this nature, and to be a great deceiver and dissembler. People are

so foolish, and such slaves of immediate needs,
that whoever fools them will always find
someone who will let himself be fooled. (XVIII-3)

One of the best-known studies of President Franklin D. Roosevelt calls him "the lion and the fox," borrowing Machiavelli's description of a leader.[15] The leonine side of an effective boss is obvious. He or she has the presence to ward off the wolves who threaten the boss or his organization with sabotage, malicious gossip, or other harm. But what about the boss as a fox? That is a less obvious idea. Yet it is clear that a boss must be enough of a fox to avoid traps: excessive flattery, phony promises, deals too good to be true, and many others. A boss must also sometimes tell the public what the majority wants to hear, even if he must stretch the truth. The majority often want to be fooled. One of America's great showmen, P.T. Barnum, made the point vividly: "There's a sucker born every minute". And even one of America's great statesmen, Abraham Lincoln, observed that "you may fool all the people some of the time; you can even fool some of the people all the time," though he added that "you can't fool all the people all the time." Machiavelli would have endorsed all three of Lincoln's observations. Despite his scientific cynicism, the man from Florence - like the man from Illinois - believed that most people seek "knowledge of honest and good things" (opening chapter, Discourses).

---

[16] James McGregor Burns, Roosevelt: the Lion and the Fox (Harcourt, Brace, Jovanovich, 1983)

A prime example of managerial foxiness, one that I have seen in every organization I have ever worked for, is job inflation. How often do bosses call even their lowliest subordinates "colleagues" or "associates"? How often does a boss hire a secretary who will not be "just a secretary" or a clerk who will not be "a mere clerk"? To be sure, such dissembling can approach absurdity, as when janitors become "sanitary engineers" and branch managers become "vice presidents".

Machiavelli again:

At some point deception becomes self-deception. The boss, therefore, need not have in fact all good qualities, but it is essential that he should appear to have them.

Indeed, I will dare to say that having them and abiding by them at all time is damaging, while appearing to have them is useful. A boss cannot invariably abide by all those principles for which people are held to be good, since it is often necessary, in order to preserve the organization, to act against faith, charity, humanity, and religion.

And yet he must have a spirit that is ready to turn according to the winds of fortune and the changes in situations, and, as I said before, be

> *good when he can, but know how to be bad*
> *when he must. (XVIII-4)*

Here Machiavelli is putting his lion-and-fox image of the leader in different terms. He argues that a boss must appear always as a pillar of virtue, but must in fact react to the "winds of fortune" as the situation requires - even if that means breaking ordinary rules of behavior. Machiavelli certainly prefers decent conduct, but he recognized that there is no choice but to break rules when the survival of the organization is threatened. Elsewhere he states: "I believe ... that it is better to act and regret than to not act and regret" (Discourses, chapter 2). How do you feel about Machiavelli's advice? Have you known bosses who follow it?

> *One very effective manager of my acquaintance*
> *exudes charm, willingness to listen, openness,*
> *and other marvelous qualities. It does not*
> *matter whether he has these qualities or not;*
> *what matters is that he appears to have them,*
> *and his employees love him for that. People also*
> *accept his tough decisions. For instance, he fired*
> *a salesman for losing a sale by being late to an*
> *appointment. When the salesman tried to*
> *explain his tardiness, the boss would not even*
> *listen, but nobody criticized him for that, since*
> *he was widely perceived to be open and fair.*

> As Machiavelli puts it:

> *A boss must, therefore, take great care never to*

say anything that is not full of good qualities, so that he appears, to those who see him and hear him, full of virtues.

All people see what you appear to be, few know what you are; and those few do not dare to contradict the opinion of those who have the power of the organization behind them; and in judging the actions of people, especially bosses, when there is no higher judge, we judge based on the results.

If a boss does well for his organization, the actions he has taken will be always judged honorable and praised; because the crowd is always attracted by appearance, and by the final outcome, and in the world there are only crowds. (XVIII-5)

All people see what you appear to be, few know what you are. Can the reader think of examples to illustrate this maxim?

I have several acquaintances who have been around a certain industry for years, changing companies from time to time, even though they are nearly totally incompetent. Their secret? They appear to be very competent, since they know well the arcane technical jargon of the industry. Many see what they appear to be, few know what they are.

To use a Vietnam-era expression: sometimes it's enough to talk the talk, you don't need to walk the talk. Although Machiavelli is realist enough to recognize the importance of appearances, he reserves his admiration for real achievements. "Nothing gives a prince more prestige than undertaking great enterprises," he writes in XXI, "and setting a splendid example for the people." When there is no higher judge, we judge based on results. Does this apply to modern business organizations?

> *A manager whom I once knew got into trouble with his new boss. He was exiled to that company's equivalent of Siberia. To everyone's surprise, his results in "Siberia" were exceptional, outstanding. Within a short time, he was back in the warm part of the world, promoted by the very man who had exiled him.*

In the world there are only crowds. A harsh judgement. Is it true? Here Machiavelli is being the hard-headed realist, while betraying some personal disappointment. In the short run, unquestionably, "nothing succeeds like success." Although *The Prince* failed to bring fame or fortune to its author during his lifetime, it brought him immortality. To be sure, Machiavelli explained elsewhere that his writing was not motivated by a thirst for fame but rather "by that natural desire that was always in me to work, come what may, for those things that I believe to be for the common benefit" (Proem to Discourses). For those who want immediate recognition - and how many mortals do not? - there are indeed only crowds. Crowds, moreover, are taken in by the trappings of success and are fickle. Where is yesterday's best-seller, Broadway hit, star real-estate promoter, or "Best Managed Firm"?

16. How Bosses can Avoid Being Despised and Hated

> *The vast majority of men live contentedly as long as no one takes their goods or their honor, so the boss needs only to contend with the ambition of few people, and this can be held in check in many ways and with ease ... The boss must arrange his actions to show greatness of spirit, wisdom, and strength. (XIX-1)*

In other words, most employees will be happy so long as their salaries and status are safe. Few will be ambitious for promotions. Machiavelli's observation was confirmed in a study of 3641 managers in 14 countries, made by a team at the University of California at Berkeley.[16] That team found that most of the managers rated security and autonomy higher than esteem. Esteem is sought only by the handful who burn with ambition.

> *I have never worked in a department where more than one or two of the employees aspired to replace the boss.*

> As Machiavelli says:

> *A boss must fear two types of conspiracies: the internal conspiracy of his employees, and the external conspiracy of other bosses. He protects*

---

[16] Mason Haire et al., Managerial Thinking: an International Study (Wiley, 1966)

> *himself against outside threats through his own competence and by having friends, and he will be secure against internal conspiracies so long as there are no successful external conspiracies. (XIX-2)*

Can a manager get into trouble with his subordinates if his peers and superiors respect him?

> *All the employees, without exception, disliked and failed to respect a certain manager I once knew - let's call him "J.R.". An unusual situation, but literally true! He had done everything possible to incur dislike and disrespect among his subordinates.*
>
> *Yet he survived for year after year, because he had the support of his peers and superiors in the organization. He had friends among them, and they knew that his operating results were good.*
>
> Machiavelli again:
>
> *But even when there are no external conspiracies, one should still fear secret internal conspiracies. These are avoided if the boss keeps his employees satisfied with his leadership. (XIX-3)*

When Machiavelli says that internal conspiracies are doomed to fail without outside support, he does not mean that such plots cannot happen. Moreover, scheming hurts productivity, even if it fails to unseat the boss. Satisfaction with the boss's leadership - not mere popularity - is the best insurance against secret conspiracies.

> As time passed, J.R. - mentioned above - had an increasingly hard time maintaining departmental productivity, because his subordinates spent inordinate amounts of time trying to figure out how to embarrass him in front of higher management.

> As Machiavelli puts it:

> I conclude, therefore, that a boss should take little account of conspiracies when the employees are on his side; but when the employees are his enemies and hate him, he must fear everything and everyone.

> Well-run organizations and wise bosses have diligently thought of ways to satisfy their employees, because doing so is one of the most important tasks of a boss. (XIX-6)

In modern business, we speak of motivating employees. How many companies have gotten into real trouble because a split developed between workers and management, and the workers were not willing to take an overall company view when the company was threatened by economic conditions or competition?

Without naming names, how about the well-known airline industry executive who was forced to step down because all of the airline's unions wanted him out, and the financial results were poor?

17. On Bosses' Behavior in Takeovers

A new boss must not demote all his employees; on the contrary, he should promote some. In this way those who suspected him become loyal, while those who trusted him become more faithful.

But if he demotes them, he offends them and shows that he does not trust them, and thus sows the seeds of hatred of the boss. Furthermore, since the new boss needs some subordinate managers, if he demotes his employees, he is obliged to bring in new subordinate managers from outside the organization, with unpredictable results. (XX-2)

Did the reader ever observe a new manager create serious morale problems by replacing all or most existing subordinate managers with his old friends from his old job?

I have seen that happen, but I would like to give a positive example instead. I mentioned before that I was once involved in a very well planned and executed takeover. One of the things we did is exactly what Machiavelli recommends: we made it a point to promote some (but not all) of the managers of the acquired organization to important jobs within our organization. This approach fostered trust and good morale in the acquired organization.

Machiavelli again:

But, when a boss acquires authority over a new organization that will be merged with his existing organization, then it is necessary to demote the subordinate managers of the new organization, except for those who were allies of the boss during the acquisition.

And even they must be made powerless over time, and a new management structure created that consists only of managers from the boss's organization. (XX-3)

How many readers have observed a corporate takeover or merger closely enough to recognize this sort of managerial problem? I have seen several such cases, and they all followed Machiavelli's observation. Note that Machiavelli's advice does not contradict the first part of this chapter, though it may seem to do so. Here he is stressing the importance of loyalty. Every organization, he says, needs key managers who are loyal to it, not to some bygone outfit. Machiavelli gives other useful advice in Chapters 1, 2, 3, and 8 for bosses involved in takeovers. When Machiavelli speaks of loyalty, he is being unsentimental as always. He is speaking of earned loyalty - not of loyalty based on old association, not even of loyalty based on past performance, but rather of loyalty based on current results.

In the smooth takeover I cited above, my outfit promoted some of the managers from the acquired organization - those who were skilled and not embittered - to key jobs in the new organization. At the same time, we filled other key jobs with tested managers from our firm - thus "colonizing" the new organization.

In addition, we gave "lateral promotions" to the mediocre people; encouraged and facilitated resignations by the malcontents; and fired the serious troublemakers. (All these stratagems are discussed in Chapters 1, 2, and 3.) While making these moves, we made sure we understood the culture of the acquired organization, its social currents, and the sources of discontent.

Machiavelli again:

Many think that a wise boss must, when he has the chance, slyly develop some enemies or problems so that, when they are defeated or solved, his reputation will improve. (XX-6)

Has the reader observed that managers whose departments never have problems are not as well respected as those whose departments have problems that are solved by the manager? Did you ever suspect that some managers cleverly foster problems that they know they can solve, just in order to get attention from higher management?

"Foster" is too strong a word, but I do know of one case first-hand (although I have never personally followed Machiavelli's advice on this point).

Resources were too thin in a certain department, and the departmental manager - let's call him "Foxy" - knew it well. He knew that higher management would not appreciate being told of this, so he said nothing, even though he had a remedial plan.

Foxy waited until performance degenerated to the point where top management got excited, and started talking about creating a special task force to solve the problem. Then he trotted out his plan for increased resources. It was approved and quickly implemented.

Performance improved dramatically, and Foxy was a hero.

Bosses have even been known to invent troublesome competitors, suppliers, or customers - preferably located far, far away from headquarters - whose mischief is overcome by the inventive bosses. Although such total fabrication cannot be recommended or condoned, exaggeration of the potency of commercial enemies or problems is natural and useful.

In many cases, the boss will easily be able to gain the loyalty of employees who were his enemies when he first took over the organization, provided that they need the support of the boss to succeed. Such employees are obliged to serve the boss well in order to dispel with actions the bad impression that they

> *know he has of them. Hence the boss will get more contributions from them, than from those who, serving him in safety, neglect his priorities. (XX-7)*

When Machiavelli speaks of enemies here, he means persons who took different policy positions, not of persons "out to get" the boss regardless of circumstances. Sooner or later, every boss finds himself in such situations. We have all read of political candidates who welcomed former opponents to their teams - even as "running mates" - and won strong support from them. I have been in the position of a boss with former opponents as my subordinates, and also in the reverse position where one of my former opponents became my boss. You may be sure that I extended myself when my boss was an ex-opponent - more so than his longtime supporters did - and that my ex-opponents extended themselves for me when I became their boss.

> *The boss who has acquired a new organization thanks to the internal efforts of that organization must consider well the reasons of those who favoured him. If their motivation is not natural affection towards him, but is merely dissatisfaction with the previous state of affairs, it will be difficult for the boss to maintain their favour, because it will be impossible for him to satisfy them.*

It is much easier for a boss to make friends of people who were happy with the previous state of affairs, and hostile to the new boss, than to maintain the friendship of people who supported a takeover because they were unhappy with the previous state of affairs. (XX-8)

Here Machiavelli is talking about the psychology of discontent. Every politician soon learns the cost of winning office thanks to "dissatisfaction with the previous rascals" rather than thanks to "natural affection" for the newly elected candidate. Dissatisfaction breeds unrealistic expectations, which no boss can satisfy. Affection implies only hope for improvement - a New Deal, in one famous phrase. The wise boss will offer hope of improved conditions but not a prescription for remedying dissatisfactions.

18. What the Boss Should Do to be Respected

Nothing creates as much respect for a boss, as his accomplishing difficult tasks and acting in a bold and dignified manner. (XXI-1)

Above all things, a boss must find ways to make all his actions appear those of a person with a great spirit and an outstanding mind. (XXI-2)

A boss is respected if he is a true friend or a true enemy, that is, if he openly shows himself for or against someone. (XXI-3)

A boss must also show himself a lover of performance, by listening to able employees, and rewarding those who have outstanding abilities. Furthermore, he must encourage his employees to improve their skills, ... and should reward whoever has ideas for improving operations. In addition he must, at appropriate times, organize parties and entertainments.

And, since any organization is divided into groups, he must take this diversity into account, and meet with each group once in a while, showing his concern and generosity, while maintaining his dignity, which must be present at all times. (XXI-7)

Note the order of Machiavelli's checklist for bosses. First and foremost is the boss's manner. Next comes the boss's general attitude, followed by his specific behavior towards subordinates. Fourth in line are incentives for improved performance. In fifth place we find social activities. Last and not least is what we now call group dynamics.

Modern psychologists confirm Machiavelli's wisdom. Consider a study of the "likableness" of key personality traits.[17] The subjects rated these five traits highest on a scale of 0 to 6: sincere, loyal, truthful, warm, friendly. Orderly and careful were a distant fifth and sixth. A boss should behave with true dignity to all, especially his employees, meaning honestly, forthrightfully, and sympathetically. Psychological studies support Machiavelli's judgement that a boss can motivate his subordinates effectively by being a good listener and by giving words of encouragement when employees behave as desired (this is known as "positive reinforcement" in modern psychological jargon, as opposed to "negative reinforcement" which consists in meting out verbal or physical punishment when undesired behavior is observed).

Ever since the famous Hawthorne studies at a Western Electric plant,[18] modern experts have recognized the importance of informal groups within the formal organization. Machiavelli saw their importance five centuries ago. A successful boss pays attention to every cohesive group - often

---

[17] N.H. Anderson, "Likableness Ratings of 555 Personality Trait Words," Journal of Personality and Social Psychology (no. 9, 1968)

[18] The Hawthorne studies were started by Elton Mayo in 1927 and are reported in F.L. Roethlisberger and William Dickson, Management and the Worker (Harvard University Graduate School of Business, 1947)

called a team - in a company, fostering their team spirit and their will to excel.

19. On the Subordinates of Bosses

The choice of his subordinates is not a matter of small importance for a boss.

Subordinates can be good or not, depending on the wisdom of the boss. The first opinion one forms regarding the mind of a boss is based on the people that surround him; when they are competent and loyal, the boss can be considered wise, because he was able to recognize competence and inspire loyalty. When they are otherwise, one can have a poor opinion of the boss, because the first mistake a boss can make is in the choice of his subordinates. (XXII-1)

Can the reader think of good managers whose departments contained good employees? And of bad managers whose departments contained poor employees? Do you see a correlation? Since a good definition of management is getting work done through other people, it is clear that choosing the right people and motivating them is a fundamental requirement for success.

The most successful organization that I ever worked for was not particularly well managed in the conventional sense (that is, in such areas as planning or making decisions swiftly). Its secret for success was to hire and retain the best people, so that their employees were always a cut above those of their competitors.

Alfred Sloan, who built General Motors, chose able and loyal lieutenants such as Charles E. Wilson (later President Eisenhower's Secretary of Defense) and Charles F. Kettering (later co-founder of a cancer research institute). By contrast, Henry Ford alienated his best subordinates and kept only yes-men. The consequences for Ford Motor Company are discussed at the end of Chapter 7 and in Chapter 10.[19]

As Machiavelli says:

There are three kinds of minds: those that reason by themselves, those that understand the reasoning of others, and those that do not reason by themselves and do not understand the reasoning of others. The first are most excellent, the second excellent, the third useless. (XXII-2)

---

[19] See GM Passes Ford: 1918-1938, by Arthur J. Kuhn (Penn State Press, 1986)

Here again Machiavelli anticipates the conclusions of modern psychology. According to one authority, "the socially valued traits which accompany originality include independence of judgment, freedom of expression, and novelty of construction and insight." On the other hand, "the socially disrated traits that may go along with originality include rebelliousness, disorderliness, and exhibitionism."[20] Clearly a boss will want only a limited number of original thinkers among his subordinates, and will want them in special positions, assigning most positions to Machiavelli's "those that understand the reasoning of others."

> Here is an infallible method for judging a subordinate. If you see that the subordinate thinks more of himself than of you, the boss, and that in all actions he seeks his own good, then you know that he will never be a good subordinate, and that he will never be trustworthy. Because whoever holds delegated responsibility should never think of himself, but of his boss.
>
> And, correspondingly, the boss, in order to maintain loyalty, must think of his subordinate, rewarding him, sharing honor and promotions, so that the subordinate will see that he depends on the boss.

---

[20] Frank Barron, Creativity and Psychological Health (Van Nostrand, 1963)

> *When bosses and subordinates act in this was, they can trust each other; when they act otherwise, things will always end badly for one or the other. (XXII-3)*

In other works the manager-subordinate relation must be a symbiotic partnership, where both gain by working together. Neither can gain on his own, and both must recognize and reward the contribution of the other.

> *I observed a case in point. A new manager stated his intention to change the way of working of a complex decentralized and matrix-managed organization. He wanted to build a team, and wanted the organization to work as a team.*

> *A good idea, but he was unable to implement it because he continued to act like a hierarchical manager; since he never treated his subordinates like team members, they never became team members, and continued to act like hierarchical subordinates. As one observer said, "They always saluted but never reported the condition of the trail ahead."*

> *The manager wanted to gain for himself the advantages of a team structure, without giving anything up to his subordinates. It was a one-way deal, and it was refused.*

20. How Bosses Should Avoid Flatterers

I do not wish to omit an important topic, an error that bosses avoid with difficulty, unless they are exceptionally able. This error is to come under the spell of flatterers, who abound in all organizations.

Because people like themselves and their own actions so well, they avoid this plague with difficulty, and those who wish to avoid it risk losing their prestige. For there is no way to avoid flattery, except to let people know that they will not offend you if they speak the truth; but when everyone can speak the truth to a boss, he loses his prestige. (XXIII-1)

Poets throughout the ages have warned against flattery and against confusing it with helpful advice. Shakespeare regretted that "men's ears should be to counsel deaf, but not to flattery!" How can a boss keep his ears open to useful advice while closed to flattery? And how can a boss avoid advice that is sound enough but is unnecessary, time-wasting, and therefore a drain on managerial authority? Here is a dilemma that is hard to solve: how to encourage subordinates to speak the truth, without losing all discipline and encouraging continual griping on minor issues?

Does the reader believe that structured methods of collecting comments are effective?

I know of one company that uses the suggestion box very effectively. A committee reviews the comments. Many are irrelevant, and are discarded. But consistently, year after year, some comments result in significant operational changes and increased profitability.

In this company, an employee who makes an accepted suggestion receives a financial reward related to the amount of increased profitability.

Machiavelli again:

Consequently, a wise boss must find another way: surrounding himself with wise people, and giving them, and only them, the right to speak the truth, and only on those topics that he has chosen; but he must ask them about all matters, and then listen to their opinions and reflect on them by himself.

With these people he should act in such a way that they know that the more freely they speak on the topic he wishes them to speak on, the better they will be accepted. Outside of them, he should not listen to anyone, nor second-guess firm decisions, and he should stand by his own decisions. Those who do otherwise will either fall prey to flattery, or will change their minds often because of the existence of many opinions; this wavering

> *creates a low level of respect for the boss. (XXIII-2)*

That is, managers must maintain a certain distance from subordinates, and must be wary of rewarding only those subordinates who always agree with them. Can the reader think of managers who have gotten into trouble by falling prey either to flattery or to excessive familiarity with subordinates? How does this trap differ from consulting a trustworthy staff?

> *I know one very talented manager whose effectiveness is severely limited by his inability to avoid flatterers. This individual's subordinates are always "yes-men," with no skills or ability to do anything except say yes.*

> *As a consequence, the manager has to do himself all the work that his subordinates should be doing. Although he is very good, no one person can be as good as an effective team, so the performance of his department is not what it should be.*

> As Machiavelli says:

> *A boss, therefore, must always obtain advice, but when he wants it, and not when others want to give it; indeed, he must discourage everyone from giving him uncalled-for advice. But the boss must ask for advice often and broadly, and patiently listen to the truth regarding the topics he has asked about; indeed, he should become*

upset if he notices that someone, out of respect, is not speaking the truth.

Now, many think that a boss who is held to be wise might have that reputation not because of his own nature but because of the good advice that he receives. There is no doubt that such people are mistaken. For the following general rule is never wrong: a boss who is not wise on his own account cannot be advised well. The only way he could be advised well would be by delegating all decisions to one very wise person. This could happen, but it would not last long, because the wise person in a short time would take the boss's place.

If a boss who is not wise takes advice from several persons, he will never get consistent advice, and will be unable to impose consistency himself; each advisor will think in his own way, and the boss will not understand and will be unable to integrate them.

It cannot be otherwise, because people will always treat you badly, unless they are forced to be good.

Therefore we conclude that good advice, from whomever it comes, must grow out of the wisdom of the boss, and that he wisdom of the boss cannot grow out of good advice. (XXIII-4)

The best managers I know are people who know what questions to ask. This is their technique for soliciting honest advice.

I have never met an effective manager who asks for general, unstructured advice. Nor have I known a successful boss who relies on a single advisor.

Recently, a business newspaper reported on the expensive failure of a large and well-known company to develop a ew type of compressor. Senior executives did not receive low-level reports on problems.

Says one top-manager now, in retrospect: "I'd have gone and found the lowest damn level people we had ... and just sat down in their little cubbyholes and asked them 'How are things today?'"

21. On Holding Power

The above precepts, correctly observed, make a new boss appear seasoned and wise, and make him quickly more secure in his position than if he had been there a long time.

For the actions of a new boss are more closely watched than those of an old boss, and when they are seen to be wise, they inspire people more than past actions. Because people are more concerned with the present than the past, and when they find good in the present, they are happy and do not seek further. (XXIV-1)

Machiavelli recognized the fact that bosses are judged by their subordinates for present performance alone. Employees are not much impressed by a boss's past triumphs, if he cannot deliver the goods today. Indeed the human race judges most individuals in this way. That hard fact causes some resentment including bitter jokes like "Yesterday you saved my life, but what have you done for me today?" Yet this psychological bias is an inescapable truth in human experience. Past performance may bring medals or honorary degrees, while only present performance evokes confidence among superiors, peers, and subordinates.

A boss that loses his power should not blame bad fortune, but rather his own incompetence. Indeed, if during good times he never thinks

> *that times might change (and this is a common failing of people: to neglect possible storms during periods of calm weather), when adverse times come, he will run away instead of defending himself. (XXIV-3)*

In other words, the time to start contingency-planning for the worst case is when things are going well. Once things degenerate, you will have no time to prepare counter-measures. Have you been in an organization confronting changing conditions?

> *Industrial history is filled with examples of failures to prepare for change. In USA in recent times, Big Steel; the Big Three auto makers; and many computer companies including Wang, IBM, and Digital are prime examples. On the other hand, some defense contractors apparently made plans, before the end of the Cold War, to cope with potential reductions in defense spending.*
>
> *A book publisher has told me of the impact of revolutionary developments in printing technology since the 1950s - he calls these the "most fundamental changes in the five centuries since Gutenberg invented printing in the 1450s." Letterpress impressions from heavy metal plates gave way to photo-offset "kissing" from expendable plates, while*

typesetting was replaced by computer composition. The few publishing managers who had prepared themselves (and their companies) for the changes had an edge over the unprepared majority.

22. The Role of Luck in Human Affairs, and How to Channel It

> *I believe it might be true that luck is decisive in half of our actions, but nonetheless we are masters of the other half. (XXV-1)*
>
> *Fortune shows her power where there is nothing to resist her, and turns her strength wherever she knows that there are no dikes or dams to impede her. (XXV-3)*

While the precise allocation of luck and skill in successful ventures is difficult or impossible to make, Machiavelli's 50-50 split is considered a good rule of thumb by many historians. Machiavelli uses the image of building dikes or dams against torrents as an example of channeling bad luck. Regarding good luck, Shakespeare also uses a watery image when he says, "There is a tide in the affairs of men, which, taken at the flood, leads on to fortune." Dutch farmers used dikes to protect their farms against unlucky flooding from the sea, while Dutch explorers and traders took advantage of flood tides when setting sail of voyages of discovery. Can you think of situations where success was due to correct exploitation of a piece of good luck?

> *Examples of success growing out of a combination of luck and know-how are legion. One case from the computer industry. A company made a great piece of hardware, but it*

was too expensive for the intended application. Then Independent software houses discovered that the high-resolution screen display of the machine could be used in new and imaginative ways to improve the human interface of their software.

Sales of the machine took off, and it became the standard hardware platform for that type of application. The company cleverly exploited this piece of good luck by realigning their marketing and positioning themselves as THE company in that field of activity.

23. On Organizations That Need Leadership

I know an organization where there is great quality among the employees, but not among the managers.

Compare these employees individually with competitors, and you will see how superior they are in knowledge, skill and intelligence. But, when compared as an organization, they cannot hold up.

This is entirely due to the weakness of the management, because those who know something are not obeyed, and everyone thinks he knows best. Up to now there has not been someone who knew how to stand out and use skill and luck to assume leadership. (XXVI-4)

Every sports fan knows that two-dozen superstars do not make a winning team without a strong coach. Conversely, strong coaches have been known to knit so-so players into an unbeatable team through the magic of leadership. Have you seen this happen in business?

The most successful leaders are both task-oriented (concerned with results) and employee-oriented (concerned with people), according to research by Robert Blake and others.[21] Machiavelli's analysis of his experience reached the same conclusion.

---

[21] Robert R. Blake, Jane S. Mouton, Louis B. Barnes, and Larry E. Greiner, "Breakthrough in Organizational Development," Harvard Business Review (winter, 1964)

Postscript:
Machiavelli's Life and Times

I. Machiavelli's Life

Niccolò Machiavelli was born in Florence, on May 3rd, 1469. His family was of noble stock and had its ancient origins in the small town of Montespertoli.

Niccolò started writing comical poems and songs in his youth, showing already that lack of concern for prejudice and convention, and that ability to observe the world as it is, that would reach its apex in *Il Principe*. Humanity should not fear, he wrote, "as if the world to its end was near" "for when the devil for real you see/with fewer horns, and not as black is he".

In June 1498 Niccolò was appointed head of the Second Chancellery of the Secretariat of the Republic of Florence. This office acted as the ministry of war and internal affairs, and reported directly to the ruling council. Republican leaders had regained power in Florence in 1494 after almost a century of rule by the Medici family.

Marcello Adriani, Secretary of the Republic, was an academic, more interested in oratory than in practical affairs, so young Machiavelli had considerably more freedom and power than would have been normal in his subordinate position in the Secretariat.

For the next fourteen years he served the republic faithfully and energetically. When he was part of a foreign embassy, he was often a non-speaking observer, preferring to let others do the talking, while he watched and learned.

In 1500 he travelled to France, to the court of Louis XII, to report on some unrest among the King's mercenary troops in Italy. He visited France three more times, after 1504, writing up his observations in the short pamphlets *De Natura Gallorum* and *Ritratto di Cose di Francia*. As in his youthful writings, he observed and reported on reality, with no regard for anyone's pre-conceived notions; the French, he wrote, "are most humble when fortune is against them, and insolent when fortune is in their favor."

In 1502 Niccolò was sent twice as envoy and observer to Cesare Borgia. Cesare's methods for increasing his power fascinated Machiavelli; he described them in the *Descrizione del Modo Tenuto dal Duca Valentino nello Ammazzare Vitellozzo Vitelli, Oliverotto da Fermo, il signor Pagolo e il Duca di Gravina Orsini*. We find these observations again, later, in *Il Principe*.

In 1506 Machiavelli was in Rome, envoy to Julius II. This strong-willed and powerful Pope also earned Niccolò's approval and admiration. The following year, he visited the court of Emperor Maximilian, and spent some time among the noblemen of the Tyrol valley, whose frugal habits he praised in the *Ritratto delle Cose della Magna*.

From 1505 to 1507 Machiavelli was secretary of the Nove della Milizia, the body in charge of recruiting and arming local citizens, in order to avoid having to depend on the unreliable and rapacious mercenaries of the time.

The year 1512 brought the Medici family back into power in Florence. Faithful servants of the republic were dismissed from office. Niccolò tried hard to stay in power, but in vain. Not even his great book, *Il Principe* (1513), was enough to impress the Medicis.

He retired to a house in the country, and devoted himself to writing. First the *Discorsi sopra la Prima Deca di Tito Livio*, then *Il Principe* and the *Dialoghi dell'Arte della Guerra*. Later, he wrote the Vita di Castruccio Castracani, a biography in which Machiavelli projects his own ideals. The Istorie Fiorentine were commissioned by Giulio dei Medici, who would become Pope Clement VII, and were composed between 1520 and 1524.

In his own time, Machiavelli's historical and political essays were not well received, but he became well known as the author of the comical play the *Mandragola* (1520), a satire in the best classical tradition. Even more popular was *Clizia* (1525), a play openly derived from Plautus.

Niccolò Machiavelli died on June 20, 1527, at the age of 58.

II. Machiavelli's Times

Turbulence, war, and homicide are the words that best characterize the world in which Machiavelli lived.

At the time, Italy was divided into numerous small states, each competing with the others for territory and power. Strong foreign armies from France and Spain intervened in the affairs of these petty states, increasing the turbulence. The two great powers fought each other, on Italian territory, for hegemony over the rich and populous kingdoms of Naples and Sicily and for control of the independent cities of the North, Milan in particular.

Bands of mercenaries roamed the country, pillaging, raping, and murdering when they were not fighting, and when their leader, the condottiere, was not trying to establish himself as the head of one of the petty states by usurping the power of the previous head. Keeping control of an Italian city-state required strong leadership.

The Pope tried to extend his own domains, continuing the centuries-long struggle with the Holy Roman Emperor for nominal sovereignty over Italy. Fierce Swiss mountaineers descended into the fertile Italian plains to conquer portions of them for themselves. Only Venice remained above the turmoil, safely isolated by the lagoons between it and the mainland, participating in the Italian wars only when it was to her advantage. Thus Venice was the commercial gateway from Asia to Europe.

In spite of, or because of, the political turmoil, great artists flourished, and produced works that we cherish to this day.

A few key events:

1494   Charles VIII, King of France, invades Italy,
and the Medici, rulers of Florence, are expelled. The Republic is proclaimed. Charles conquers the Kingdom of Naples, but is soon forced to abandon it by a league comprising the Pope, the Emperor, King Ferdinand of Aragon, and others.

1497   Leonardo da Vinci paints the Last Supper.

1498   The Dominican monk Girolamo Savonarola,
demagogic leader of the democratic party in Florence, is excommunicated and burned at the stake. Charles VIII, King of France, dies and is succeeded by Louis XII. Machiavelli starts his political career.

1499   With the aid of French troops, Cesare Borgia,
son of Pope Alexander VI, becomes Duke of Romagna.

1501   Michelangelo Buonarroti sculpts the David.
Louis XII, King of France, and Ferdinand, King of Aragon, conquer the Kingdom of Naples.

1503   Pope Alexander VI dies and is succeeded by
Julius II. End of Cesare Borgia's power.

1504   Death of Isabelle, Queen of Castile. French
expelled from Naples. Ferdinand of Aragon and Castille assumes full power.

1505   (approx.) Leonardo paints La Gioconda
(Mona Lisa).

1506	Bramante designs the new Basilica of St. Peter in Rome.
1508	Michelangelo starts to paint the ceiling of the Sixtine Chapel. Raphael Sanzio starts to decorate the Stanze in the Vatican.
1509	Henry VII, King of England, dies and is succeeded by Henry VIII.
1510	The Holy League is formed by the Pope, King Ferdinand of Aragon and Castille, and others, in order to expel the French from Italy.
1512	The Medici return to power in Florence, as a result of the victories of the Holy League. Machiavelli's political career ends.
1513	Pope Julius II dies and is succeeded by Leo X, a Medici. The Swiss defeat the French at Novara.
1514	Death of Bramante.
1515	Louis XII of France dies and is succeeded by Francis I. Francis I defeats the Swiss at Marignano and conquers Milan.
1516	Ferdinand, King of Aragon and Castile, dies and is succeeded by his son, Charles I (later Emperor Charles V).
1519	Death of Leonardo. Death of Emperor Maximilian. He is succeeded by Charles V.
1520	Death of Raphael.
1521	Emperor Charles V claims Milan, and starts a long series of wars with Francis I, King of France.

1525	Francis I defeated and captured at the battle of Pavia.
1527	The Medici are again expelled from Florence. Michelangelo, elected member of the Nove delle Milizie, works on improving the fortifications of Florence. Machiavelli dies.

THE FALL OF UBS

The Forces That Brought Down Switzerland's Biggest Bank

Dirk Schutz

ISBN 0-944188-20-6

"UBS CEO's Fall from Grace Tells a Tale of Euroland" **Wall Street Journal**

"Why did Cabiallavetta, the CEO of the Union Bank of Switzerland, agree to such a deal?" asked The Economist on January 31, 1998. The deal was a merger between UBS and Swiss Bank Corp., a smaller rival. One reason, **The Economist** speculated, was that there was, "in UBS's London based derivatives business, a hole of unknown (but possibly huge) proportions."

What happened at UBS is a complicated story involving power, ambition and vanity. It shows that risk management controls in the largest of the Swiss banks had not extended far enough from the experience. And the responsibility for the failure falls principally on Cabiallavetta.

Essential reading for business and finance professionals: a complicated story of power, ambition, vanity and a lack of risk management controls at one of Europe's largest banks.

A bestseller in Europe: already over 35,000 copies sold. No. 1 on bestseller list in Europe for seven months!

AIR GUIDE for the Frequent Flyer

The Official Guide to the World's Airlines and Airports

Edited by Aram Gesar

ISBN 0-944188-14-1

"Air Guide is a new one stop source for travelers seeking basic facts on more than 100 of the world's major airlines and airports. There is a mine of information on airline fleets and services - seating, food, entertainment, shopping and frequent flyer programs. You can check how much legroom you can expect in all classes - even which seat rows offer most room."
International Herald Tribune

The *Air Guide* is filled with tips and advice and provides the traveler with everything he needs to know to make intelligent decisions before, during and after travel. Exhaustively researched, with comprehensive information to help the traveler reserve the most comfortable seat, avoid losing luggage, find the best frequent flyer program, understand airline aliances, even reduce the effects of jet lag.

Air Guide provides indispensable, up to date information on air travel and over 100 international airlines and airports, including travel tips and advice, airline ratings and reviews. *Air Guide* is the first of its kind. This guide is the one to have on hand for your next business trip, vacation, or other travel experience.

THE INTERNET TRAVEL GUIDE

Surf the Web and Travel Right.

Edited by Kimberley A. Strassel

ISBN 0-944188-17-6

Here's the guide to launch you into cyber travel space. How to navigate the web to make all your travel arrangements and save time and money.

The Internet Travel Guide presents the best in combining travel and technology. Instead of suffering through the formidable information in travel cyberspace this book will guide you to the sites that offer clear, concise and essential data.

Travelers now have instant access to a rapidly expanding galaxy of user-friendly systems that allow to plan and book all their travel simply by pointing and clicking with a mouse. This timely guide will give hands-on advice on how to make the best use of the Internet to navigate the travel Web sites easily to save time and money, plan and book one's own travel, book airline tickets, air taxi, helicopter, hotel rooms, rental cars, cruises and casinos, check for deals and steals.

About the author: Kimberley A. Strassel has been the assistant editorial features editor for the Wall Street Journal. and for the Wall Street Journal Europe.

ONLINE PUBLICATIONS
AIR GUIDE for the Frequent Flyer Online
www.AirguideOnline.com
The Official Guide to the World's Airlines and Airports.
Also available in print and CD-ROM.
Updated monthly.
This indispensable reference guide for the frequent flyers
packed with up-to-date, detailed information on international
airlines, airports and travel. Exhaustively researched, with
comprehensive information to help the traveler reserve the
most comfortable seat, avoid losing luggage, find the best
frequent flyer programs, airline alliances, even reduce the
effects of jet lag, the AIRguide provides everything the
traveler needs to know to make intelligent decisions before,
during after travel.

Travel Monthly Articles
(travel advice, money saving and practical tips)
Travel Tips & Information
(check lists, must/never do, health and jet lag tips)
Travel Deals (airline, around the world and hotel deals)
Travel News
Travel Links
Airport & Destination
Airport Information & Services
Destination Information
Airlines
Airline Class of Service
Airline Reviews & Comments
Airline Ratings
Airline Ground & In-flight Services
Airline Aircraft Seating
Airline Fleets
Airline Frequent Flyer Programs
Airline Lounges
Airline Reservation Telephone Numbers

ORDERING INFORMATION

Our titles are sold in the United States, Canada, United Kingdom, Europe and Asia

Single Copy or Bulk Sales, Trade Discounts & Sales
Corporate & Special Sales, Co-Publishing
Advertising Sales
E-Mail : info@pyramid.ch
Orders : orders@pyramid.ch
Rights & Permissions : rights@pyramid.ch

PYRAMID MEDIA GROUP, Inc.

North America
666 Fifth Avenue, Suite 230
New York, NY 10103, USA
For Orders :
Tel : +1 800 626-4330 Fax : +1 800 334-3892
Europe
CP 635, Geneva Airport,CH 1215, Switzerland
Tel : +41 22 343-1111   Fax : +41 22 343-0220

TRADE DISTRIBUTION
Distributed in North America by :
LPC Group Sales
1436 West Randolph Street, Chicago, IL 60607, USA
Tel : +1 800 243-0138 / 626-4330 Fax : +1 800 334-3892

Represented in the UK, Europe, Mid-East, Africa, Asia & Australia by :
Chris Lloyd Sales & Marketing
463 Ashley Road, Parkstone, Poole, Dorset BH14 0AX
Tel : +44 1202 715-349   Fax : +44 1202 736-191

For Orders :
ORCA Book Services (formerly Cassell Distribution)
Stanley House, 3 Fleets Lane, Poole, Dorset BH15 3AJ.
Tel : +44 1202 665-432   Fax : +44 1202 666-219
E-Mail : orders@orca-book-services.co.uk